DYING
TO KNOW

DYING
TO KNOW

RAM DASS & TIMOTHY LEARY

Edited by **Parvati Markus**

Based on the film by **Gay Dillingham**

MANDALA

SAN RAFAEL LOS ANGELES LONDON

To Ram Dass and Timothy Leary for bravely sharing
their minds and hearts with us so we could be here now
and think for ourselves with unconditional love

CONTENTS

FOREWORD

BY GAY DILLINGHAM

AS I WRITE THE FOREWORD for this book, I am looking back at an extraordinary, life-changing journey—the making and sharing of the film *Dying to Know*. Like many others on this path, I have always been curious, dying to know more about the Great Mystery, the final frontier we call death. And so, for a few years after the film was released, we held conversations with audiences after screenings in approximately a hundred communities across the country. Our grassroots team of Zach Leary, Michael Donnelly, and myself were joined by leaders from the hospice movement, drug policy, and consciousness communities. We were able to spotlight many of the scientists from Johns Hopkins, UCLA, and NYU, who were coming out with groundbreaking studies on the therapeutic use of psychedelics in the treatment of addictions, PTSD, major depression, end-of-life issues, palliative care, and more.

Rather than going immediately into digital distribution, I wanted people to come to the film, so we could gather together around a modern campfire, tell our stories, and contemplate our futures. In the dark of theaters, without interruption from our daily routines, we shared our hearts and minds in a contemplative, sacred space. People of all ages traveled hours to get to theaters, or came back for second or third viewings so they could bring family and friends. As Leary might say, we were helping to ease some of the fears associated with the unknown "just by talking about it" in the right "set and setting."

In the face of Leary's approaching death, Ram Dass and Timothy Leary held a conversation that lives on in the film, and now in this book. Join the conversation! Talk with your friends and family and community. Explore the philosophical, psychological, and spiritual dimensions that weave through the hopes and fears we have surrounding death and dying. Stand with Ram Dass and Timothy Leary, the pioneers of mind expansion, by going into the heart cave that Ram Dass talks about, and taking Tim's advice to *think for yourself.*

And may the time you spend with these giants of consciousness bear fruit in your own life.

INTRODUCTION

BY PARVATI MARKUS

WHETHER YOU'VE heard of them or not, the epic friendship of these two complex, controversial characters—Timothy Leary and Ram Dass—changed your life and those of a generation, and beyond. Together and separately, they ushered in an awakening of consciousness through the psychedelic revolution and Eastern spirituality. Here we will explore their lives and their relationship, from their fateful meeting at Harvard to the divergence of their lives in different directions—Ram Dass as a spiritual teacher, Tim Leary as the "Pied Piper of LSD" and proponent of cyberspace.

ABOVE: Harvard Reunion, 1983.

This book is based on Gay Dillingham's film *Dying to Know: Ram Dass & Timothy Leary*, which premiered at the Mill Valley Film Festival in California in October 2014. It was a labor of love, which started on a whim in 1995 while Gay and her husband at the time, Andrew Ungerleider, were at dinner with friends Sandra Hay and Alan Kozlowski, where the news of the day was being discussed: Timothy Leary had announced he was dying. They realized it was a historic moment, so Andrew said, "Let's get Ram Dass to come down from San Francisco for a final goodbye with Tim." The baby boomers around the table knew the importance of their relationship and their place in history.

Gay was thirty years old when Tim announced he was dying. She had been born after Timothy Leary and Richard Alpert, the Harvard psychologist who morphed into Ram Dass, had been fired from Harvard. She had seen Leary once when he was doing the college lecture circuit in the '80s during his cybertech and software design period and had not been impressed by his showmanship. And, like many others, she had read *Be Here Now* while in college, the "hippie bible" written by Ram Dass. Now she found herself drawn to these two men because of her own exploration of death.

Gay, the youngest of four children, was very close to her brother Matt, three years her senior. At the age of twenty, when Gay was in high school, Matt died when he accidentally lost control of his car on a mountain road. His death shook her world. Psychedelic mushrooms helped her slowly reignite her spirit, the flame that had almost gone out when Matt died. In an interview for this book Gay said, "At Matt's burial, I realized how constipated our culture was around death. I sat there and watched my brother, who loved nature, get put in a cast-metal casket down into a metal casing. *Oh my God, he's never gonna get back!* That was my first visceral awareness of death. We are so upside down about death and have such an inability to keep it on our shoulder so that life is more precious."

After the dinner party, Andrew got Leary's attention by sending him a gift certificate for Jack Kevorkian. Known as "Dr. Death," Kevorkian championed a terminal patient's right to die by physician-assisted suicide. Leary thought the gesture was hysterical, so he said, "I'm in."

Then Andrew called Ram Dass (unbeknownst to both of them at the time, they were cousins) to get him to come down from the Bay Area to join Tim in conversation. Ram Dass complained he didn't have time to do it because he was on a deadline for his book on aging (ironically titled *Still Here*). Andrew responded with what he knew would get Ram Dass, "You sound attached."

Ram Dass laughed, "You got me. I'm in."

ABOVE: Gay and Ram Dass.

MAKING THE MOVIE

When Gay arrived at Leary's house to start setting up the cameras, she saw a sign on the front door: Mother of All Parties. The scene was wild. The house was filled with young people who honored Tim as a pioneer in cyberspace, a coffin with Yoda in it, and paraphernalia around cryonics. At the time, Leary was still thinking about doing cryonics, until Nena (one of his former wives) and Bob Thurman dissuaded him from freezing his brain.

In her role as director, Gay's goal was to create the "set and setting," so after giving Ram Dass the questions and topics she wanted him to cover, she got the cameras rolling, and tried to disappear so as not to interrupt the men's conversation. It was risky, but it created gold. After the filming was finished, Gay was pulling her hair out in the editing room trying to find cut points in their freewheeling, overlapping conversation. There was so much context she didn't understand that she spent the next years doing research, in between launching an environmental technology business and doing government work on environmental management for the state of New Mexico on problems ranging from climate change regulations to nuclear weapons and mass extinction—an immersion in death and planetary dying.

Gay was fortunate to get a final solo interview with Tim shortly before he died, and a solo interview with Ram Dass in the narrow window right after Tim died in May 1996 and before Ram Dass's debilitating stroke in February 1997. In 2012, when she was deep in working on the film, Gay interviewed others whose lives intersected at different points with Leary and Ram Dass: Dr. Andrew Weil, an international best-selling author and founder and director of the Andrew Weil Center for Integrative Medicine; Huston Smith, influential professor of religion and author of *The World's Religions*; Roshi Joan Halifax, author and founder and abbot of Upaya Zen Center in Santa Fe, New Mexico; Ralph Metzner, PhD, author, psychologist, and Harvard contemporary with Leary and Alpert; Joanna Harcourt-Smith, former common-law wife of Leary; Lama Tsultrim Allione, author, Tibetan Buddhist lama, and founder of Tara Mandala, an international Buddhist community and retreat center in Pagosa Springs, Colorado; John Perry Barlow, rancher, Grateful Dead lyricist, and cofounder of the Electronic Frontier Foundation; Peggy Mellon Hitchcock, resident, owner, and benefactor of the Hitchcock Estate in Millbrook, New York; and Zach Leary, Timothy Leary's son.

Gay spent time with Ram Dass after his stroke; she watched him over the years evolve into someone who learned to live in unconditional love. The stroke was the fulcrum in the middle of his spiritual life. After the stroke, the transmission he had received from his guru, Maharajji (Neem Karoli Baba), about being in the heart, loving and serving everyone, opened him more and more fully over time until he was resting in a state of unconditional love. Although Gay respected Ram Dass's relationship with Maharajji and was glad for him that he had that, it wasn't until she attended a retreat on Maui in 2018 that she got Maharajji. As Ram Dass was introducing the love of Maharajji to each person at the retreat, Gay felt Maharajji's picture behind Ram Dass come to life, animated with pure love that she experienced throughout every cell of her body, especially in her heart.

Gay sat for years with the material she had gathered. Her father died. Big things were happening with her business and the government work. She finally put together a rough cut of the film and shared it with Chuck Blitz, an old friend of Ram Dass. Chuck sent Gay flowers and said, "You must finish. This film is too important and beautiful."

The more time went on, the more Gay realized the story was relevant not only to her own life but also to the American psyche. Like many in her generation, she had inherited caricatures of these two men and needed to reconcile their portrayal in the media with who they were as people. In Leary, the man she met on his deathbed, she found an intelligent, searching, vulnerable, honest, complex human being—a natural risk-taker breaking conventional boundaries for what he believed could bring about a higher level of consciousness. He was somewhat naïve, paid dearly for it, and she

grew to love him. Over the years, as she got to know him better, Ram Dass became a guiding light for Gay. Although his body had been ravaged by his stroke, with pain as his constant companion, he consistently practiced unconditional love until his own death in December 2019. Gay is grateful she had time to let her dream world and the collective unconscious work on it. She believes the film made her as much as she made the film.

THE RAM DASS–TIMOTHY LEARY RELATIONSHIP

After so many intense shared experiences and so much time together in the early years, Ram Dass and Leary grew apart and developed in different directions—Leary as a visionary intellectual and social revolutionary, Ram Dass as a spiritual teacher and Eastern philosopher. A 1983 Harvard reunion rekindled the friendship between these controversial figures, who had broken the societal taboos on sex, drugs, and death.

They danced in, out, and through each other's complex lives for decades until, ultimately, Leary's terminal cancer inspired the 1995 meeting arranged by the filmmakers. Ram Dass was the first person Tim called when he found out he was dying. Gay knew that the relationship between these two larger-than-life men could fulfill her original goal to have a deeper conversation about the final human frontier of death.

On the first day of filming, before the cameras were set, Ram Dass and Tim arrived and were hugging by the front door. Gay could immediately sense the magic of their connection. Death does seem to bring people to their truths, and there was a lot of transformation with Tim as he approached that threshold with honesty, fear, and the tremendous curiosity that was a big part of who he was as a person.

Tim and Ram Dass had such beautiful symmetry, with Tim as the yang and Ram Dass as the yin, the heart. But the beauty of the yin-yang symbol is that inside the yang is the yin, and in the yin is the yang. Tim had a very big heart and Ram Dass had a very big intellect. After the shooting was over, Tim said, "Thanks for bringing us together so we could make love in public."

When Gay interviewed Ram Dass the summer after Tim had died and before his stroke, Ram Dass had been thinking deeply about his relationship with Tim, their cosmic buddy journey. Ram Dass spoke the truth about Tim, but through the lens of love rather than judgment. Tim has been both so glorified and so demonized by the culture that it was the first time she felt like she could understand Tim's story. Our media culture wants to judge, but Gay decided the film would tell the truth through love. Together and apart, these two men put psychedelics back into medicine and opened the culture's consciousness in a way that one could practice and live into expanded awareness.

At multiple conferences on psychedelics, many of the speakers would start their talk with some version of, well, if it wasn't for Timothy Leary screwing it up, legitimate research in psychedelics would have continued. But the genie had gotten out of the bottle, as it would have no matter what Tim did or didn't do. Millions of people have done psychedelics and had positive experiences with them that changed their lives, which would not have happened without Timothy Leary as the Pied Piper, the evangelical, and Ram Dass for creating the open, loving environment.

FROM A MOVIE TO A BOOK

Usually, it's a book that gets turned into a movie. Here, we're turning a movie into a book so you can enjoy at leisure the photos and graphic art from the film as well as having the time to contemplate the concepts discussed in the film that come out of the relationship between Ram Dass and Timothy Leary and their extraordinary lives and deaths.

This story is much larger than a simple conversation between two old friends. Through the arc of their entire lives, we see how two Harvard professors became counterculture icons. We explore their upbringing, early life, and their fateful meeting at Harvard, where together they ran fully sanctioned experiments into the nature and use of psilocybin and LSD until 1963, when Ram Dass was fired for giving a psychedelic drug to one undergraduate student and Leary's contract was not renewed for "failure to keep classroom appointments." Supporters compared Alpert's dismissal from Harvard to Ralph Waldo Emerson having been fired a hundred years earlier for promoting the idea that one has direct access to God. We follow them from Harvard to Millbrook, where their experimentation continued and where their friendship was tested and fractured. They both then went their own way—one to India, one to prison—each becoming a legend in his own right.

In the conversation Gay recorded for posterity, both men share openly their thoughts and perspectives as they rekindle the love they have always felt for one another. Both were

TIM AND RAM DASS
HAD SUCH BEAUTIFUL
SYMMETRY, WITH
TIM AS THE YANG
AND RAM DASS AS
THE YIN, THE HEART.

more than willing to bring death out into the open—an empowering entrance into the mystery of the beyond. And here you, the reader, are free to dive deep into the questions prompted by their encounter: What role does the brain play in consciousness? Is the ego death of the psychedelic experience the same as physical death? What is unconditional love? What happens after death? We are all dying to know.

It's interesting to have a film about death that is inspiring, curious, and hopeful. During the two years of its first-run theatrical release, in over eighty theaters across the country, Gay invited in people involved with drug policy, hospice, medical research with psychedelics, etc., and hosted community conversations where people could express their feelings and thoughts around death and psychedelics. Ram Dass and Leary held such remarkably different perspectives about death that it allowed in everyone's point of view, from the philosophical materialist "You're dead when you're dead" to the spiritual optimist, "Consciousness keeps happening after you die; the soul goes on." Who knows if either one is right or wrong, but let's engage the mystery and have these conversations. Let's bring in more consciousness around death, both ego death and physical death. Let's bring light to our minds and joy to our hearts as we share the hearts and minds of Ram Dass and Timothy Leary.

As Ram Dass said, "We're all just walking each other home."

PREFACE

THE NEWS THAT TIM WAS DYING

IN THE SUMMER of 1995, Timothy Leary announced to the world media that he had been diagnosed with inoperable prostate cancer. He was dying. In December, Gay Dillingham filmed the two together . . . for the last time.

ABOVE: Timothy Leary and Ram Dass, 1995 film footage.

RAM DASS: *Hey you, you blew society away when you talked about how you were looking forward to death.*

TIMOTHY LEARY: *Which society?*

RAM DASS: *The society you and I have lived in . . .*

TIMOTHY LEARY: *Oh, there are several societies.*

RAM DASS: *Suddenly the AP was calling me. They said, "Did Timothy say he had good news for you when he told you he was dying?" I said yeah. They said, "What did you say?" I said, "I'm happy." There was a silence on the phone.*

TIMOTHY LEARY: *Good for you!*

RAM DASS: *I said I was delighted.*

TIMOTHY LEARY: *Well, yes, that's why you're the first person I called, because I knew you would understand.*

RAM DASS: *But why do you think the society's blown away so much by that?*

TIMOTHY LEARY: *It's the taboo of all time. Right now there are only a few more taboos. We knocked off the taboo against sex.*

RAM DASS: *Well, you did personally. [laughter]*

TIMOTHY LEARY: *Remember how obsessed society got about drugs? It still is. War on drugs? We certainly know about that taboo.*

RAM DASS: *Yeah, sure. So, the next thing is death.*

TIMOTHY LEARY: *Ultimate taboo.*

RAM DASS: *You know, I was thinking about it on the way down here. I was thinking of you as the great escape artist.*

TIMOTHY LEARY: *Sure.*

RAM DASS: *And this is what you're doing now. You're escaping from something or other.*

TIMOTHY LEARY: *But I'm also going towards the ultimate fear.*

RAM DASS: *Well, you're going through the ultimate fear.*

TIMOTHY LEARY: *Remember when people used to say that LSD is an escapist drug?*

RAM DASS: *No, it's not escapist. It's confrontation.*

TIMOTHY LEARY: *And my thing about death is not escaping it. I'm running towards Miss Death.*

RAM DASS: *No, I think that the way you're running is an escape from the cultural values that say you should push against it.*

TIMOTHY LEARY: *As a reverence thing, yeah.*

RAM DASS: *When I think about the moment of death, I usually think of a great acid trip. I think of the disillusion of conceptual structures.*

TIMOTHY LEARY: *Yeah.*

RAM DASS: *And then I feel you're catapulted out into nonconceptual space. Is that the way you're imagining it?*

TIMOTHY LEARY: *Exactly. It's the classic mind, mind, mind. Get the mind outta there 'cause nothing happens till you can quiet your mind. Once you put a saying into your mind, it's like a drunken monkey . . .*

RAM DASS: *I stole that line; it was not mine. I stole it from an old Indian.*

TIMOTHY LEARY: *They had all the good lines.*

RAM DASS: *That's what I read the holy books for . . . to get good lines.*

WE'RE OLD BEINGS THAT KNOW EACH OTHER WELL THROUGH MANY FORMS.

TIMOTHY LEARY: *I'm an opportunist. I ride these waves of the culture and everybody has deep thoughts about death. And, of course, the Catholic Church says don't worry, priests will take care of you. You can't turn it over to the priests. You can't turn this over to the doctors. You can't turn it over to the medical profession. Think for yourselves. Take charge of it! Plan it! Talk to your friends about it. No government agency or no profession can solve these problems for you. I've got to do it for myself. You've got to do it for yourself.*

* * *

TIMOTHY LEARY: *It's a very funny situation. I'm dealing with doctors. I want to be a good patient. And my doctors, they're reading the paper every day. So, I walk into the office and in one day two doctors criticize me . . .*

RAM DASS: *For saying you were happy about dying?*

TIMOTHY LEARY: *Well, he says we're gonna keep you alive, see?*

RAM DASS: *That's their Hippocratic oath. They can't help it.*

TIMOTHY LEARY: *Hypocritical oath, man.*

RAM DASS: *They see death as their enemy . . . Staying with the dying business for a while, what kind of rituals could you imagine? How would you break out of the cultural fear of dying? What is your statement doing and what else could be done? What else could we do? Hospice was a big jump over the intensive care unit.*

TIMOTHY LEARY: *Yeah.*

RAM DASS: *And now we've gotta do more jumps. Are you ready?*

TIMOTHY LEARY: *I like that. Jump.*

TIMOTHY LEARY: *When you walked in, there was a flash of total joy.*

RAM DASS: *Yeah, yeah, me too.*

THINK FOR YOURSELVES. TAKE CHARGE OF IT! PLAN IT! TALK TO YOUR FRIENDS ABOUT IT. NO GOVERNMENT AGENCY OR NO PROFESSION CAN SOLVE THESE PROBLEMS FOR YOU. I'VE GOT TO DO IT FOR MYSELF. YOU'VE GOT TO DO IT FOR YOURSELF.

TIMOTHY LEARY: *And love. Just joy.*

RAM DASS: *See, in my mythology now I say you and I are connected at a place where we both dance through this incarnation together, but we have a connection that is timeless in another sense, like we're old beings that know each other well through many forms.*

TIMOTHY LEARY: *Who are you? Who am I? It's a very difficult question. Throughout my life I've always been fascinated by where the action was. I never wanted to have power, but I ran for governor once against Ronald Reagan. I wanted to experience the different theaters or stages or viewpoints of life. I think I've lived one of the most interesting lives of anyone in the twentieth century.*

RAM DASS: *I think my incarnation is wonderful. I mean, I started out a Jewish boy from Boston, from psychology to psychedelics to Eastern mysticism, and then to have ended up Ram Dass, aaah . . . just getting straight on towards God.*

BIRTH

TIMOTHY LEARY

TIMOTHY LEARY was born October 22, 1920, in Springfield, Massachusetts, to Timothy "Tote" Leary, a dentist, and Abigail Ferris. He was the only child of his Irish Catholic parents.

ABOVE: Timothy Leary in March 1996, two months prior to his death.

RAM DASS: *He took birth into such an interesting tension. On his mother's side, very conservative Irish Catholic, very held in tight, very judgmental. And his father was from the Learys, who were kind of a wild, Irish, drinking, divorcing, going-off-and-running-away type of family.*

When he was thirteen, Tim's abusive, alcoholic father handed him $100 and took off. Tim didn't see him again until twenty-three years later. His paternal grandfather, Dennis Leary, liked the boy because he, unlike the rest of the family, really liked to read. He told Tim never to be like anyone else, to find his own way and be one of a kind. Like his grandfather, Leary would never do anything by half. And like most of the men in the Leary clan, Tim inherited both their Irish charm and their recklessness.

TIMOTHY LEARY: *I was a heavy reader as a child. I spent hours and hours as a kid studying the heroic and the interesting and the adventures of people who were thinking.*

RAM DASS: *Timothy had an extraordinarily complex and subtle mind. He liked the multilevel nature of consciousness a lot. I mean, the fact that James Joyce was one of his favorite writers is certainly a key, a clue. He was the romantic Irish bard, also the kind of itinerant scholar, the kind of rascally person at the bar. And he seemed to play the role of that kind of guy.*

HUSTON SMITH: *What he was at heart was an Irish rebel.*

WHAT HE WAS AT HEART WAS AN IRISH REBEL.

TOP: Leary with his mother, Abigail. **ABOVE LEFT:** Leary with his father, "Tote." **ABOVE RIGHT:** Leary, the student.

ROSHI JOAN HALIFAX: *Like a good Irishman, he could just pull tricks out of the bag. And he did it continually.*

ANDREW WEIL: *He had a twinkle in his eye and seemed leprechaunish and mischievous.*

After high school, Leary was kicked out of three colleges, including the US Military Academy at West Point, where his reputation for breaking the rules and drinking binges took firm hold when he was court-martialed for supplying liquor to other cadets. Getting kicked out of places would become a hallmark of his life.

RAM DASS: *There was a thing about Timothy about right and wrong; that he was busy being a bad boy, but in the rascally sense, the playful sense. Timothy was not mean spirited. He was absolutely quite the opposite.*

JOHN PERRY BARLOW: *As Aldous Huxley said of him, "The good Dr. Leary would serve our cause and his own better if he could resist his impulse to cock snooks at authority." There was a thing in Tim that just liked to piss people off.*

When he lost his student deferment in the midst of World War II, Leary was drafted into the US Army. He was on the noncommissioned officer track, enrolled in the psychology studies of the Army Specialized Training Program. Briefly assigned to a war-bound group, he called it (in his autobiography *Flashbacks*) "a suicide command . . . whose main mission, as far as I could see, was to eliminate the entire civilian branch of American aviation from post-war rivalry." Finally, he got an honorable discharge.

FROM TOP TO BOTTOM: Huston Smith, Roshi Joan Halifax, Dr. Andrew Weil, John Perry Barlow.

While posted to the Army Medical Corps hospital in Pennsylvania, Leary met and married Marianne, his first wife, in April 1945, and in the next four years they had two children, Susan and Jack.

Becoming a family man seemed to kick-start his ambition. Leary completed his college degree via correspondence courses in August 1945. A year later, he received his master's degree in psychology at Washington State. By 1950 he had earned his PhD in clinical psychology from UC Berkeley. He went on to cofound Kaiser Hospital's Psychology Department in Oakland and to direct research at the Kaiser Foundation Psychological Research Center.

Leary was known as the founding force behind transactional analysis, in which the psychologist engages with the patient as an equal (a concept that proved important later on when guiding psychedelic trips). Leary did clinical research at Berkeley and was published widely in respected journals. He devised a personality

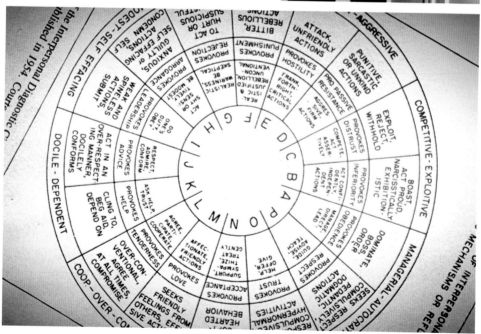

TOP: Leary's children, Jack and Susan. **CENTER:** Leary teaching. **ABOVE:** The Interpersonal Behavior Circle.

LIKE A GOOD IRISHMAN, HE COULD JUST PULL TRICKS OUT OF THE BAG.

TOP: Leary at West Point. **ABOVE LEFT:** Leary in the U.S. Army. **ABOVE RIGHT:** Marianne and Timothy, married 1945.

HE TOLD TIM NEVER TO BE LIKE ANYONE ELSE, TO FIND HIS OWN WAY AND BE ONE OF A KIND.

ABOVE: Leary and his first wife, Marianne.

LEARY WAS KNOWN
AS THE FOUNDING
FORCE BEHIND
TRANSACTIONAL
ANALYSIS, IN WHICH
THE PSYCHOLOGIST
ENGAGES WITH
THE PATIENT AS AN
EQUAL (A CONCEPT
THAT PROVED
IMPORTANT LATER
ON WHEN GUIDING
PSYCHEDELIC TRIPS).

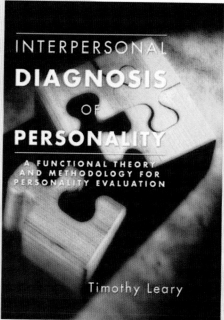

TOP LEFT: Leary, the young professional.
TOP RIGHT: Leary's first book. **ABOVE:** David McClelland.

test—the Interpersonal Behavior Circle—which was so highly regarded that it was used by the judicial system to evaluate prisoners. Years later, when Leary was imprisoned for possessing a small amount of marijuana, he was given the test he had designed himself. He answered the questions to show he was unlikely to bolt, so he was assigned to be a gardener in the minimum-security wing, which set up the possibility of his escape.

Even though his professional life was thriving, his personal life was a mess, filled with alcohol (he and Marianne were both heavy drinkers), infidelity, and despair. After hearing that Tim was having an affair, Marianne, who suffered from severe depression, committed suicide on the morning of his thirty-fifth birthday in 1955.

He was left with two young children and a ton of Catholic guilt. In *Flashbacks*, Leary described himself as "an anonymous institutional employee who drove to work each morning in a long line of commuter cars and drove home each night and drank martinis and looked like and thought like and acted like several million middle-class, liberal, intellectual robots."

In 1957 he published his first book, *Interpersonal Diagnosis of Personality*, which was called "perhaps the most important clinical book to appear this year" by the *Annual*

Review of Psychology. When his contract was not renewed, he moved to Europe with his children. A colleague from Berkeley, Frank Barron, met Tim in Florence, Italy, and mentioned he had taken "magic mushrooms" and had mystical insights.

Tim said, "I was a bit worried about my old friend and warned him against the possibility of losing his scientific credibility if he babbled this way among our colleagues."

Barron introduced him to David McClelland, chairman of the Center for Research in Personality at Harvard, who was in Florence on sabbatical at the time. McClelland was impressed by Leary's desire to throw out the old doctor-patient model in psychological study and get involved with his subjects in real-life situations, and he invited Tim to Harvard.

RICHARD ALPERT

RAM DASS started out as Richard "Dick" Alpert, born on April 6, 1931, to Gertrude and George Alpert in Boston, Massachusetts. The youngest of three boys, he was the beloved baby of the house, the family mascot. His mother came from a wealthy family (her Russian immigrant father had business relations with Louis B. Mayer, who went on to become the head of MGM Studios).

In classic Jewish mother mode, she used food as love. When Richard learned she had given birth to him against medical advice because of a blood condition (which later developed into leukemia), he felt she had sacrificed herself for him, so to please his mom he ate and ate until he was overweight. His complex relationship with his mother was one of the reasons he went into the study of psychology and did years of Freudian analysis. He was harassed at school and called a "fat, dirty Jew." His brother Billy called him "Satchel Ass."

Besides his weight, which finally disappeared when he went away to prep school, he had another problem: He was attracted to boys. At prep school, some upperclassmen caught him wrestling naked in his room with another kid, and afterwards no one would be seen with him. Ostracized from the other students, he had no one he could talk to about it. "Sexuality wasn't anything you talked about in the 1940s, certainly not in my family." Years later he would learn he had at least three cousins on his mother's side who identified as homosexual.

> **RAM DASS:** *I kept a front up because I'd be scorned. You just didn't talk about homosexuality. I mean, my prep school, boy, I went through hell internally. My homosexuality set the stage for feeling like an outcast.*

> **ROSHI JOAN HALIFAX:** *You know, I feel like we're all straight, we're all gay. We all experience some kind of social rejection; we're all kind of confused. We're all, to some degree, imposters, people with feet of clay. Psychological analysis or*

TOP: Richard Alpert. **CENTER:** Richard with his mother, Gertrude. **ABOVE:** Richard as young student.

psychosocial analysis of Ram Dass's gayness is for me simplistic. Part of it is the privilege that he was brought into. Part of it is the fact that he was the third son. Bodhidharma was the third son of a king, and he became a big outlier in the community of Buddhism. Part of it is the timing of his birth. So many things conspired to bring him forward on the path that he ended up pursuing. I don't think of Ram Dass as gay or straight. It's kind of interesting. I don't really assign a gender to him, a preference to him. He's gay. He's straight. It might have been a key variant in his life that made him really move into the position of an outlier. There's a lot of suffering around sexual identity in our culture.

Home was filled with music. His mother played piano. His father had a dance band and string quartet and played the violin. His brother played the organ. Richard played cello and would emcee at musical fundraising events held at his home. It was music that gave Richard his first experience of death. His uncle Mickey was an orchestra leader who was doing just that at the Cocoanut Grove in Boston in 1942, when the deadliest nightclub fire in US history killed nearly 500. Mickey escaped through a bathroom window and came to the Alpert home, sobbing. Richard was eleven and realized that none of the adults could talk comfortably about death.

TIMOTHY LEARY: *When we met, it's true I had read more of the books, but you were ten times more streetwise than I was.*

RAM DASS: *Really?*

TIMOTHY LEARY: *Yeah.*

RAM DASS: *I always think of myself as kind of a nebbish, you know, [laughter],*

I KEPT A FRONT UP BECAUSE I'D BE SCORNED. YOU JUST DIDN'T TALK ABOUT HOMOSEXUALITY. I MEAN, MY PREP SCHOOL, BOY, I WENT THROUGH HELL INTERNALLY. MY HOMOSEXUALITY SET THE STAGE FOR FEELING LIKE AN OUTCAST.

ABOVE: George Alpert, president of the New York, New Haven, and Hartford Railroad.
LEFT: George Alpert and Albert Einstein.

lost soul, very square, and you picked me up. I mean you helped me [laughter].

TIMOTHY LEARY: *Well, you were also a very scared Jewish boy . . .*

RAM DASS: *Yes, I was also that.*

Richard could breathe free during summers spent at Willenrica, the family's "gentleman's farm" in Franklin, New Hampshire. A boy's paradise, it boasted a three-hole golf course, a big fruit and vegetable garden, a nearby lake for water sports and the family's sailboat, a tennis court, and a barn filled with Ping-Pong tables, a shuffleboard court, and an old-fashioned foot-pedal letterpress, on which they printed labels for his dad's raspberry jam holiday gifts.

His father was concerned with money and status. George was an assistant district attorney and then started a law firm with his brother (Alpert & Alpert), which took them through the Great Depression. Later he became president of the New York, New Haven and Hartford Railroad. George was also involved in Jewish charities and was president of the temple board that hired and fired rabbis.

Along with Albert Einstein and others, George helped to found Brandeis University at a time when the Ivy League schools accepted only a small quota of Jews, and he became chairman of the board of the university and a school trustee.

TOP: Seated: George Alpert. Standing, left to right: brothers Richard, Leonard, and Bill Alpert. **ABOVE:** George, Gertrude, and Richard.

THERE HE WAS: A HOMETOWN SUCCESS IN A BIG CORNER OFFICE AT THE AGE OF TWENTY-SEVEN . . . WHEN LEARY ARRIVED AT HARVARD.

George would have preferred Richard study medicine, preferably at Harvard. A law or business degree would also have been okay. But Dick couldn't get into Harvard, and his father didn't think he should go to Brandeis because the professors would have a hard time grading the chairman's son. Instead, he graduated from Tufts University in 1952 with a degree in psychology. The outsider feelings he'd had since prep school prompted his interest in the study of the mind and behavior. This was followed by his master's in psychology at Wesleyan, where his mentor was David McClelland. McClelland recommended he attend Stanford for his PhD, which he received in 1957.

While getting his PhD, Alpert lived a bicoastal existence: He was on the faculty at both UC Berkeley and Stanford in California, then flew to the East Coast to help his father at the railroad three days a week. Another double life was his pursuit of both male and female lovers. And yet another was the daytime academic teacher and therapist versus his nighttime involvement with the beat generation. He'd drive to San Francisco's North Beach at night and hang out at City Lights Bookstore to hear the Beat Generation poets and writers. It was there that Allen Ginsberg's openness about spirituality and homosexuality changed Dick's buttoned-up East Coast perspective, and Alan Watts introduced him to Eastern philosophy.

On the East Coast, Alpert became close friends with the McClellands and lived with them for a while in their big house in Cambridge, right near Harvard. Mary McClelland was an artist and loving presence. A contemplative Quaker, she was the first truly spiritual person Dick ever met, and opened him to the possibility of an inner life.

When David McClelland started teaching at Harvard, he helped Alpert get a tenure-track position as an assistant professor in clinical psychology. There he was: a hometown success in a big corner office at the age of twenty-seven . . . when Leary arrived at Harvard.

LIFE

HARVARD UNIVERSITY

TIMOTHY LEARY: *When I went to Harvard there was another young professor, who was a very lovable, charismatic person, and we joined up as a team. Richard Alpert, who is now Ram Dass, was more conservative.*

RAM DASS: *When I was at Harvard with Timothy I was so gung ho. I had appointments in four departments simultaneously, and also research contracts at Stanford.*

RALPH METZNER: *Dick was fantastically successful; I mean he had appointments at Stanford and Harvard, and then he had a plane, and he had a car. He was like a shining star. He had tremendous charisma.*

ABOVE: Dr. Timothy Leary and Dr. Richard Alpert, Harvard professors.

At the Center for Research in Personality, on 5 Divinity Avenue in Cambridge, Massachusetts, Alpert helped with research, taught psychology, advised undergrads, and on the administrative side wrote grants and assigned office spaces. While firmly in the closet himself, he was a psychotherapist at Harvard University Health Services who wound up as the therapist for all the homosexual students. Unlike freewheeling San Francisco, homosexuality was treated as a psychological disorder in Boston.

Dick played the Harvard power game, with the big corner office, three secretaries, and numberless research assistants. His apartment in Cambridge was filled with antiques, and he had a Triumph motorcycle, an MG sports car, a Cessna airplane, and an imported Mercedes-Benz sedan. At the same time, he cruised gay bars, had a girlfriend on one side of Boston, and a boyfriend on the other.

ANDREW WEIL: *I was an undergraduate at Harvard between 1960 and 1964. I had met Dick Alpert at a party. I found him uncomfortable to be around. He seemed to not be comfortable in his own being.*

One day Dave McClelland said, "Dick, we have a new guy coming in. Can you find him an office?" And there was Timothy Leary. There were few office spaces left in the department, but three doors down from Alpert's big corner office was a room no bigger than a closet, which became Tim's domain in September 1959.

> TIMOTHY LEARY: *I was given the hottest big office at the time. I looked around. It was right next to David McClelland. And I said, "I don't want to be here," and they said there was a broom closet. It was not quite a broom closet.*

RAM DASS: *It was close to a closet. I had one of those big corner offices, if you recall.*

TIMOTHY LEARY: *I know you did.*

RAM DASS: *And you saved me from my big corner office.*

The two men were the only faculty members who held evening office hours, and so they got to know each other.

TIMOTHY LEARY: *I remember I'd be working late at night and drinking. Sometimes there'd be a line of graduate students wanting to sign up with you. Remember that?*

I WAS LIKE MR. POWER PLAYER IN ACADEMIA.
TIMOTHY WAS WAY OUTSIDE OF THAT.
OF ALL THE COLLEAGUES AROUND ME, HE
FRIGHTENED ME BECAUSE HE WAS SO FREE.

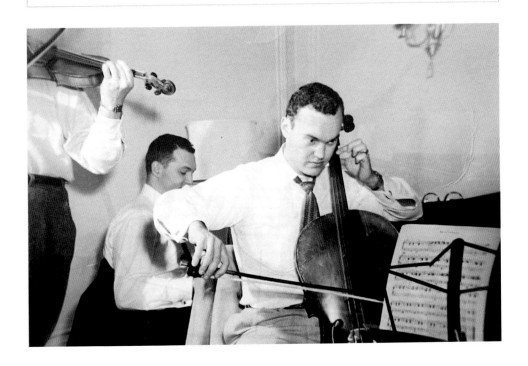

RAM DASS: *What, are you cleaning it up? [laughter] Young boys waiting to come into my office, as I recall. Yes. Well, I had a very active life, yes.*

TIMOTHY LEARY: *And I did learn a lot about sexual freedom from you.*

RAM DASS: *And I from you.*

TIMOTHY LEARY: *Because I had been a serially menigamous . . . menigamous? Monogamous. There's a song about that: iggamus, bigamous, monogamous.*

RAM DASS: *Serially monogamous, you were.*

TIMOTHY LEARY: *Yeah. There was always one.*

RAM DASS: *One. They might come in very close proximity, but there was always one at a time.*

TIMOTHY LEARY: *Yeah. My average marriage . . . I've had seven and three-quarters marriages.*

RAM DASS: *Well, forget the marriages. In between marriages, I remember a very active period in your life at Millbrook, for example.*

TIMOTHY LEARY: *Oh, yeah. Well, yeah.*

Leary described Alpert (in Robert Greenfield's biography of Leary) as an "ambitious academic-politician—engaging, witty, a big tail-wagging puppy dog." What Alpert noticed was that Tim was unusual, from the white sneakers he always wore to the fact that, unlike everyone else at Harvard, he wasn't impressed by being there.

TIM WAS LEADING A GRADUATE SEMINAR ON EXISTENTIAL TRANSACTIONALISM, A MAJOR RETHINKING OF RELATIONSHIPS USING THE LANGUAGE OF GAME THEORY. HE WANTED PSYCHOLOGISTS INVOLVED WITH THEIR PATIENTS AS RESOURCES, NOT AS AUTHORITY FIGURES—A REVOLUTIONARY CONCEPT.

ABOVE: Leary in his office at Harvard.

RAM DASS: *I saw you were laughing at the system, you know, and I had no sense of humor whatsoever.*

TIMOTHY LEARY: *You're not supposed to laugh at Harvard and Judaism.*

RAM DASS: *I know, and there was nobody else at Harvard laughing at it but you. There was nobody else that was laughing. Who? Who was laughing? Even David McClelland wasn't laughing.*

TIMOTHY LEARY: *If it doesn't have a sense of humor, I don't think the greater powers are very interested in them.*

RAM DASS: *You were the one who showed me that it was possible to escape from the system. You know, you really did. I mean it's been hard for me to understand how I was ready to hear that even. You sort of spoon fed me through it.*

TIMOTHY LEARY: *Oh, that's a nice—a Jewish mother. I'm proud to be it, okay? Here's to your mom.*

RAM DASS: *Shall we drink to your mom, too?*

* * *

RAM DASS: *Timothy was the only consciousness on the faculty that hadn't been so impressed with being at Harvard. Later, my guru said about temples, "What do I want with a pile of bricks?" And that's the way Timothy saw Harvard, as a pile of bricks. Harvard is so somebody-ness, it's so self-important. And for him*

TOP: Leary enjoying "the Harvard game." ABOVE: Dick as a young power player.

to laugh at that . . . how did he get to the point where he could laugh at it all? Why hadn't he been co-opted?

Leary and Alpert started teaching courses together on psychotherapy and game theory. Tim liked to talk about "the professor game" or "the Harvard game." Tim was leading a graduate seminar on existential transactionalism, a major rethinking of relationships using the language of game theory. He wanted psychologists involved with their patients as resources, not as authority figures—a revolutionary concept. Alpert delighted in Leary's mind and the two started hanging out together after work.

RAM DASS: *I was like Mr. Power Player in academia. Timothy was way outside of that. Of all the colleagues around me, he frightened me because he was so free. I began to sense what a visionary was; that Timothy had the ability to see outside of systems, and therefore he could open things to where you'd go, but it would take you a while to get there, maybe, and he was doing that for me.*

In the spring of 1960, Alpert was headed to Stanford to help gather data on new ways of doing math. Once he finished the research, he would fly down to Mexico to meet Tim in Cuernavaca. Dave McClelland had rented a house ten miles away to finish writing his book *The Achieving Society*. Frank Barron, a pioneer in the psychology of creativity, and other academics would be there. Frank had been talking incessantly about the insights he'd gotten from magic mushrooms, but Tim was against drugs.

Until he got curious . . .

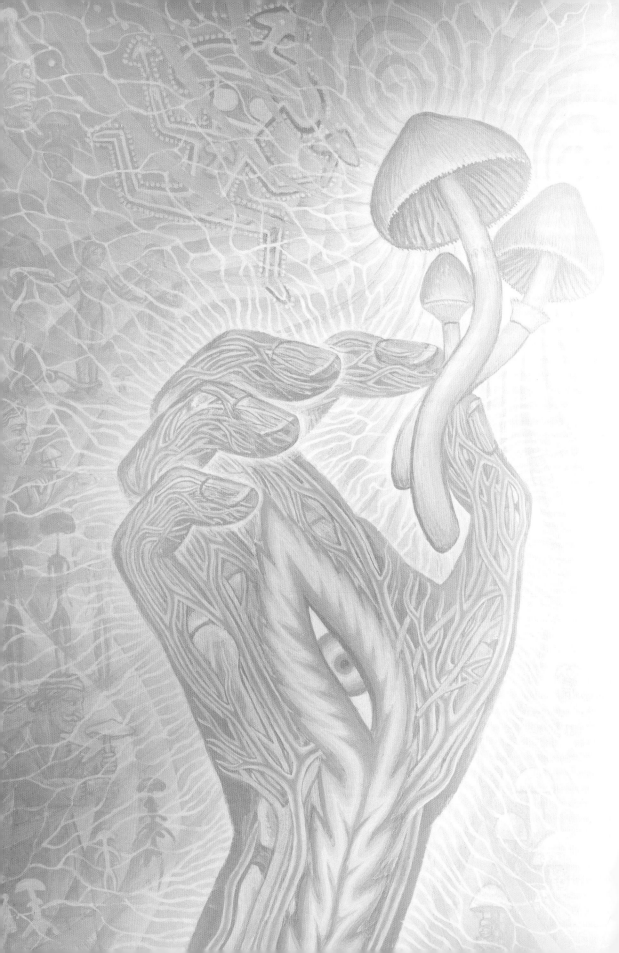

FLESH OF
THE GODS

HUSTON SMITH: *He said here, take these.*
They're interesting.

The sacred mushrooms grow on the slopes
of volcanic peaks of Mexico. On August 9,
1960, Crazy Juana, a local *curandera*
(medicine woman) with severe curvature
of the spine and gray, stringy hair, delivered
the teonanácatl mushrooms, the flesh
of the gods. The mushrooms had been
rediscovered in 1955 by R. Gordon Wasson,
a banker, author, and ethnomycologist. Then

ABOVE: Tim's book, *The Politics of Ecstasy*.
OPPOSITE: Painting by Alex Grey.

in 1957, the British psychiatrist Dr. Humphry Osmond, who coined the term *psychedelic,* and
the visionary author Aldous Huxley visited Wasson to hear him speak about the mushrooms.

Wasson's account was published in *Life* magazine (May 13, 1957), in an article called
"Seeking the Magic Mushroom," which was the story that inspired Frank Barron to find
the mushrooms.

Leary was next to step onto the psychoactive path. Tim was about to turn forty
years old and felt his joy in life, his creativity, and his sexuality were all going downhill.
He was ready to take the magic mushrooms offered to him by a visiting East German
anthropologist, who had heard of their use among the Aztecs. Tim sat by the pool at his
villa in Mexico and looked at the dark, wrinkly 'shrooms, which he said stank of "forest
damp and crumbling logs and New England basement." He chewed his way through seven
of the sacred mushrooms.

In *The Politics of Ecstasy,* he wrote: "I could look back and see my body on the bed.
I relived my life and re-experienced many events I had forgotten. More than that, I
went back in time in an evolutionary sense to where I was aware of being a one-celled
organism. All of these things were way beyond my mind . . . the discovery that the human
brain possesses an infinity of potentialities and can operate at unexpected space-time
dimensions left me feeling exhilarated, awed, and quite convinced that I had awakened

IT WAS THE CLASSIC
VISIONARY VOYAGE,
AND I CAME BACK A
CHANGED MAN. YOU
ARE NEVER THE SAME
AFTER YOU'VE HAD
THAT ONE FLASH
GLIMPSE DOWN THE
CELLULAR TIME TUNNEL.
YOU ARE NEVER THE
SAME AFTER YOU'VE
HAD THE VEIL DRAWN.

from a long ontological sleep. A profound transcendent experience should leave in its wake a changed man and a changed life."

In his first autobiography, *High Priest,* Tim described it this way: "It was the classic visionary voyage, and I came back a changed man. You are never the same after you've had that one flash glimpse down the cellular time tunnel. You are never the same after you've had the veil drawn." To the others in Mexico he had tripped with that day, he said, "We're all schizophrenics now and we're in our own institution. But for the first time I understand James Joyce."

Alpert arrived in Mexico the following day. Tim told him, "I learned more about my brain and its possibilities and more about psychology in the five hours after taking these mushrooms than in the preceding fifteen years of studying and doing research." Alpert was impressed. Since all the mushrooms were gone, Tim promised Dick he'd have his chance back at Harvard.

Tim drove to McClelland's rented home to tell him about the mushrooms. He later realized how impossible it was to convey the experience of going into altered states to anyone who hadn't been there themselves. Tim talked about his experience with Frank Barron, who did understand, and they agreed to start a research project at Harvard. Barron would look at the effect of psychedelics on creativity while Leary worked on using the drug to bring about behavioral change. Eventually they got David McClelland's approval, and the Harvard Psilocybin Project took birth.

> **HUSTON SMITH:** *Leary was the brightest psychologist at Stanford University, but Harvard lured him away by offering him a three-year research project. He didn't have to teach at all. All he had to do was to research something important in psychology. Having an open book on research, anything he wanted to do, he, of course, wanted to research these substances.*

THE HARVARD PSILOCYBIN PROJECT

AS SOON as Tim arrived back in Cambridge, he ran into George Litwin, a graduate student who knew about mescaline (the psychedelic agent of the peyote and San Pedro cacti, used by Native Americans in their religious ceremonies for thousands of years). Leary was his academic advisor and knew Litwin was giving patients mescaline at the Massachusetts Mental Health Center. Tim had previously disapproved

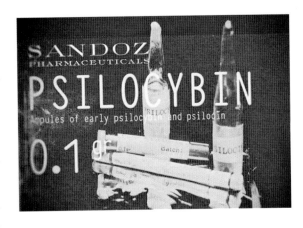

of chemically induced states and had told George to stop his drug research, but now that he understood what George had been talking about, he felt that they should start research at once. Could he help?

George could. He told Tim about synthetic psilocybin (the active ingredient of magic mushrooms) from Sandoz Pharmaceuticals. Tim immediately wrote to Sandoz for a supply. Without even asking for formal research protocols, they sent Tim a big bottle of research-grade pink psilocybin pills. All they wanted in return was a report of the results.

Tim spun out a fantasy on how he wanted to proceed. People would take turns and observe one another, keeping records of what they experienced during the session. There would be no diagnosis, no experiment results. They would test as many diverse people as possible, from housewives and cab drivers to poets, musicians, and behavioral scientists. Litwin then asked Tim if he had read any of the literature. When Tim said no, Litwin immediately handed him Aldous Huxley's *The Doors of Perception* and *Heaven and Hell*, which recounted Huxley's experiences with mescaline.

PEGGY HITCHCOCK: *I heard about these two professors at Harvard who were offering to give people psilocybin in return for having them write about their experiences. I arranged to have a session with Richard. I felt very comfortable with him, so this could only be a positive experience. It really confirmed a lot of things that I had*

IF THE DOORS
OF PERCEPTION
WERE CLEANSED
EVERYTHING
WOULD APPEAR
TO MAN AS
IT IS, INFINITE.

—WILLIAM BLAKE

hoped were true, that I had sort of glimpsed at various times in my life. In other words, there was a kind of a larger reality than what my everyday humdrum experiences were.

ANDREW WEIL: *I read about mescaline, I think after I graduated from high school, and was fascinated by it. I read everything I could and wanted to try it. When I got to Harvard, Aldous Huxley had come to MIT to give a series of lectures on visionary experience. I found out that Leary and Alpert were teaching at Harvard and were interested in this, so I went over and made an appointment. I met Leary. I had a good conversation with him. He told me that he thought these drugs were the most interesting thing he'd ever found, and the potential was enormous. He didn't see any downside to them. I asked him if I could be a subject in his research and he told me that they had made an agreement with the university that they couldn't use undergraduates. So I got a supply of mescaline*

TOP: Peggy Mellon Hitchcock. **ABOVE:** Andrew Weil, student at Harvard.

independent of anything to do with them. I took it a number of times with a group of friends of mine who were undergraduates and had variable experiences. One quite powerful one, but I didn't know what to do with that. It seemed to me if I followed the implications [of that experience] I would drop out of college, and I didn't want to do that, so I think I boxed all that up and set it aside.

HUSTON SMITH: *The first thing they did in their experiments was to mount a project in which volunteers would take the substance, and their only obligation was to write in not more than one page what they experienced. That confronted Tim with a problem because, overwhelmingly, they were describing mystical experiences and Tim didn't know beans about mysticism.*

The Harvard Psilocybin Project was widely supported and above reproach. The drug was legally obtained from Sandoz and the project was authorized by Harvard. Leary set up a research program to investigate the effects of psilocybin. Staff members trained as guides and took the drug alongside volunteer subjects in specially prepared, supportive settings. This approach became known as "set and setting." Careful evaluations were made of each session.

AFTER THEIR SESSIONS,
SUBJECTS REPORTED MANY
COMMON PERCEPTIONS:
BARRIERS DISSOLVED;
EVERYTHING SEEMED ALIVE,
EVEN INANIMATE OBJECTS;
THEY FELT A "ONENESS"
WITH EVERYTHING.

PSYCHEDELIC SESSIONS
will be conducted in these eastern-midwestern cities.

Conducted by
Timothy Leary, Ph.D. and Ralph Metzner, Ph.D.

The aim is to produce a psychedelic or ecstatic
without using drugs. The methods involve an intense
inundation of programmed stimuli — sensory, emotion

OPPOSITE: *Mycelium Dreaming* by Autumn Skye.

After their sessions, subjects reported many common perceptions: barriers dissolved; everything seemed alive, even inanimate objects; they felt a "oneness" with everything. Colors and solid patterns were transfixing, mesmerizing. The experience seemed to come in waves.

ANDREW WEIL: *When researchers like Alpert and Leary published positive results of these drugs, other researchers who didn't understand set and setting thought the magic was all in the substance. They tried to reproduce those findings and didn't get the same results. It's not just giving the drug to a person; it's giving the drug with the right expectation and the right setting.*

I don't think Leary fried his brains. I have not seen people who've fried their brains with psychedelics. I've seen people who were mentally disturbed who used a lot of drugs, but I don't think that was the cause of them. But the comment that Leary did fry his brain has been a disservice to valid psychedelic research. People who were committed to exploring the positive potential of psychedelics felt that the notoriety Leary had generated, and the immense cultural backlash that he produced, made it impossible to do legitimate research with psychedelics until quite recently. Leary could not stop himself from making comments that pushed people's buttons; he took some pleasure in that.

PSYCHEDELIC REVELATION

AFTER RETURNING to Harvard after a semester at Berkeley, Dick had dinner with his parents in Newton, Massachusetts, on March 4, 1961, and then walked over to Tim's house in Newton Centre. While Dick had been in California, Tim had launched the Harvard Psilocybin Project with Frank Barron. Tim, who had read and reread Aldous Huxley's books about his mescaline experiences, asked Huxley to be an advisor, and Huxley introduced Tim to Huston Smith, a professor of Asian philosophy at MIT who had just published *The Religions of Man*.

Huxley also introduced Tim to Humphry Osmond, a British scientist doing psychedelic research in Canada, looking at psychedelics as a way to cure alcoholism. Osmond connected Tim to the poet Allen Ginsberg, who had been part of the government LSD trials in Menlo Park,

OPPOSITE: Painting by Martina Hoffmann.

California, and Ginsberg introduced Tim to writers and musicians like Jack Kerouac, Robert Lowell, Dizzy Gillespie, Thelonious Monk, and Maynard Ferguson. Tim gave psilocybin to anyone who asked in exchange for a report on their experience.

Leary told Alpert that his mushroom research followed in the tradition of William James, who, in the late 1800s, had studied altered states of consciousness with the use of nitrous oxide and established Harvard's Psychology Department (originally tied to the Department of Philosophy). Now it was Alpert's turn.

At Tim's house, Dick found Allen Ginsberg at the kitchen table, and the three men each took a small dose of psilocybin, which initially felt like a strong pot high. A few hours later, Alpert went off by himself to reflect on what he had felt. This is how Richard (as Ram Dass) described it in *Be Here Now*: "A deep calm pervaded my being... Then I saw a figure standing about 8 feet away ... I peered into the semi-darkness and recognized none other than myself,

I REALIZED THAT ALTHOUGH EVERYTHING BY WHICH I KNEW MYSELF, EVEN MY BODY AND THIS LIFE ITSELF, WAS GONE, STILL I WAS FULLY AWARE!

in cap and gown and hood, as a professor. It was as if that part of me, which was Harvard professor, had separated or disassociated itself from me." He let that part of himself go.

The figure changed into him as a social cosmopolite, and that went too, as did all his different aspects as cellist, pilot, lover, etc. Then he saw the figure become Richard Alpert–ness, his basic identity. What would he do without being Richard Alpert? He let go of that, too, reassured that he still had his body. But then that went!

"The panic mounted, adrenalin shot through my system—my mouth became dry, but along with this, a voice sounded inside—inside what, I don't know—an intimate voice asked very quietly, and rather jocularly, it seemed to me, considering how distraught I was, ' . . . but who's minding the store?' When I could finally focus on the question, I realized that although everything by which I knew myself, even my body and this life itself, was gone, still I was fully aware!"

In ecstasy, he ran out into the snowstorm, went back to his parent's house, and started shoveling the walk.

RAM DASS: *As professor went and middle-class boy went and pilot went, and as all of my games were like going off into the distance, I got this terrible panic because indeed I was going to cease to exist. And I got the panic, which is the panic that precedes the psychological death, because indeed Richard Alpert was dying at that point. And the panic was, "No, stop, stop! I've gotta hold on to something so I'll know who I am." And Timothy, the wise old Timothy, always says something like, "Trust your nervous system."*

TIMOTHY LEARY: *One of the most touching moments in visionary history. This man was illuminated at Newton Centre, and it was snowing a little bit. I was chasing the snow.*

RAM DASS: *Allen [Ginsberg] was there then, wasn't he?*

TIMOTHY LEARY: *Yeah. And you went home at dawn. And you were shoveling . . .*

RAM DASS: *. . . snow . . .*

TIMOTHY LEARY: *. . . snow in front of your mother and father's house. And they said, "What are you doing out there? Where the . . ."*

RAM DASS: *Yes. They said, "You idiot, come in. It's five in the morning. Nobody shovels snow."*

TIMOTHY LEARY: *And you said, "I love you, Mom," or something like that.*

RAM DASS: *I said, "I love you" and went back to shoveling snow. You freed me at that moment from my mother. That's what you did.*

TIMOTHY LEARY: *I didn't do that.*

RAM DASS: *You did!*

TIMOTHY LEARY: *The drugs . . .*

RAM DASS: *You freed me; you gave me the drug. You enticed me . . . Not enticed me, you told me what the possibility was. And I trusted you. I trusted you.*

TIMOTHY LEARY: *It was Aldous Huxley that told me. Alan Watts was a great teacher.*

RAM DASS: *Wasn't he? Wasn't he?*

TIMOTHY LEARY: *We were so lucky. You get the friends you deserve. We deserved Huxley and Watts.*

RAM DASS: *I was thinking about that quality in you where you play with the edge all the time and go right in front of the big wave. Right where society isn't quite awake to itself yet. And you walk in there and blow it apart, and then go on to something else.*

ABOVE: Richard with mother, Gertrude.

TIMOTHY LEARY: *It's going to happen anyway.*

RAM DASS: *I know, I know. Exactly. You're just running ahead of the wave.*

TIMOTHY LEARY: *I didn't create the wave. I was warning people, saying, "Enjoy it, man."*

RAM DASS: *People aren't enjoying life very much, still.*

TIMOTHY LEARY: *I don't think so.*

RAM DASS: *You are.*

TIMOTHY LEARY: *I am.*

RAM DASS: *I am, and you obviously are.*

TIMOTHY LEARY: *Oh boy, yeah.*

RAM DASS: *But I don't think most people are.*

TIMOTHY LEARY: *I know. We've done our best.*

HE TAUGHT ME TO PLAY WITH LIFE RATHER THAN BEING PLAYED UPON BY LIFE.

RAM DASS: *The basic thing that [Tim] taught me was—and I keep saying it over and over again because I've only really understood it recently—he taught me to play with life rather than being played upon by life. And that's a big difference. What he was showing me was a place of my consciousness. He helped me escape, basically. He helped me escape from a cult—my acculturation. He didn't escape from the culture; he didn't want to leave the culture. He just wanted to be free of the way the culture socializes you so that you begin to see reality a certain way.*

HUSTON SMITH: *I met Tim through Aldous Huxley. I was becoming interested [in the psychedelic experience], and I asked him, "Well, I would like to have something close to the beatific vision myself."*

Aldous said, "I suggest that you phone a professor at Harvard." And he wrote down Leary's name and also his telephone number.

With kind of a sly twinkle in his eye, Leary said, "How about New Year's Day?"

After coffee and pleasantries, Leary sprinkled a few pills on the table and said, "One is a mild dose. Two is an average dose. Three is a large dose." I cautiously took one.

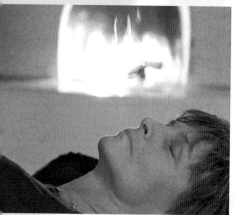

TOP: Painting by Martina Hoffman. **LEFT**: Woman in psilocybin session.

As you well know, you can't very well describe this to those who have not inhaled, as the famous phrase goes now. With every step that I took, I went higher and higher, and the vibrations in my body and my excitement and the mysteriousness of it mounted.

Later, Tim asked me, "Have you met Richard Alpert?" And I said, "No." And he said, "A very, very interesting man," which of course is true. Tim was a good writer, but Alpert was the speaker. Alpert had good sense and Leary did not. Aldous [Huxley] said to me once, "Tim is as handsome and as charming and as charismatic as anyone I have ever met. But why oh why does he have to be such an ass?"

There were three related substances: LSD, psilocybin, and mescaline. I wanted to discover whether the effects of these three differed. My conclusion was there is no difference, that the substances can alter the mind experiences, but there's no evidence that it changes behavior. Borrowing a phrase from Richard Alpert, who said, "When you get the message, hang up," so I hung up, and I have not had any ingestions since then. The object is not altered states but altered traits of behavior. Are you more kind? Are you more compassionate? And I concluded that they were powerful in altering states but zero in altering traits. And it was the latter that interested me, so that's why I hung up.

After his own experience with psilocybin, Alpert joined the Harvard Psilocybin Project, and helped Tim pull together a team of graduate students to help, including George Litwin, Ralph Metzner, and Gunther Weil, a Fulbright Scholar. Set and setting became the guiding principle of the many sessions they ran in their exploration. Both the environment in which the sessions took place and the mindset of the participants were equally important in a psychedelic journey. Intention and an attitude of openness were also important as people worked through their personal stuff and awakened to love. William James had called it *introspectionism*—studying the mind from the inside out. They kept notes of the sessions and designed studies.

Psilocybin is a unifying drug, softening the ego, opening the heart. And the doses were small, with trips lasting only three or four hours. For Alpert, psilocybin was a doorway into spirit, shared with other souls, while Leary was focused not on the mystical aspects, but on the social potential. In Leary's utopian vision, he believed it could lead to transformation of behavior and help people solve their problems.

> **TIMOTHY LEARY:** *Well, in the drug literature, going back to William James and Harvard people a hundred years ago, they always said it was the dying experience, it's the death experience. There's that classic mystic thing of joy and wonder, but I'm not advocating drugs, boys and girls. It's like anything else that's complicated. I'm very cautious. I've taken almost every drug that there is, but the reason I can survive as well as I do is because I'm prudent and I'm careful and I try to find out what's involved.*

THE CONCORD PRISON EXPERIMENT: PRISONER REHABILITATION PROJECT

The opportunity to get some hard data came from a study of the rehabilitation of prisoners. Tim used his Irish charm on the warden and the prison psychiatrist, W. Madison Presnell, at the Massachusetts Correctional Institute at Concord. Their hope was to help the prisoners break through the habits that kept getting them rearrested. Before agreeing to the study, Presnell took psilocybin himself. Every time he closed his eyes, he traveled someplace else, which is where the word *trip* came from. He agreed to see if a six-week program with two psychedelic sessions of psilocybin could bring about behavioral changes in convicts and reduce the recidivism rate (which was around 70 percent).

Presnell said (in *High Priest*), "Your plan to give psychedelic drugs to prisoners is the best idea I've heard for dealing with an impossible problem. . . . There's one chance in a hundred you can pull it off, but if you do, you will have accomplished more for American society and for prisoner rehabilitation than has been done in the last four thousand years since the code of Hammurabi. . . . Because one thing I've learned as a prison psychiatrist is that society doesn't want the prisoner rehabilitated, and as soon as you start changing

IT WAS SOON GLARINGLY OBVIOUS WHO HAD GOTTEN THE PSILOCYBIN—SOME WALKED AROUND THE CHAPEL MURMURING PRAYERS, SOMEONE CHANTED A HYMN, WHILE THOSE WHO HAD BEEN GIVEN THE PLACEBO SAT QUIETLY LISTENING TO THE THREE-HOUR SERVICE.

prisoners so that they discover beauty and wisdom, God, you're going to stir up the biggest mess that Boston has seen since the Boston Tea Party."

As the psychedelic sessions continued at the prison, strong bonds developed between the Harvard psychologists and the convicts; they guided each other through mushroom trips of joys and tears, terror and ecstasy.

The Concord Prison Experiment lasted two years and seemed to have some promising results, but nothing conclusive about the psilocybin itself, and little change in recidivism. The warmth and support of the group that had bonded in their psychedelic journeys was lost in the cold and lonely existence that was life on the outside. But there must have been an impact on the prisoners who took the psilocybin, as several of them came to pay their respects to Tim on his deathbed.

THE GOOD FRIDAY EXPERIMENT

Walter Pahnke, who had a medical degree and was a PhD candidate in the philosophy of religion at Harvard, proposed a double-blind experiment to see if psychedelics could bring about an authentic religious experience, which would be the basis of his thesis dissertation.

Walter Houston Clark helped find twenty volunteer subjects from the Newton Theological Institution. On April 20, 1962, at Boston University's Marsh Chapel, half the group was given psilocybin while the other half received a placebo. No one was told what to expect. It was soon glaringly obvious who had gotten the psilocybin—some walked around the chapel murmuring prayers, someone chanted a hymn, while those who had been given the placebo sat quietly listening to the three-hour service. The next day, those who had taken a trip reported classic mystical experiences. The Good Friday Experiment, also called the Miracle of Marsh Chapel, would be the Harvard Psilocybin Project's most public event.

> **HUSTON SMITH:** *There were sixteen of us in this small chapel who had ingested. I very soon felt the awe coming over me.*

> **TIMOTHY LEARY:** *It was probably the greatest Good Friday in 2,000 years.*

Meanwhile, David McClelland and other Harvard faculty were growing skeptical of the scientific validity of the so-called research, which didn't seem like good science to them since it was based on highly subjective experiences rather than measured and repeatable behavior. As Ram Dass said in his autobiography *Being Ram Dass*, "Love and peace and personal growth are not the stuff of conventional scientific inquiry."

People were starting to wonder what was happening at Harvard.

LSD

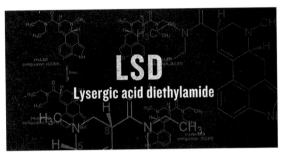

OPPOSITE: Painting of Albert Hofmann by Robert Venosa.

LSD (lysergic acid diethylamide) was first synthesized by the Swiss chemist Albert Hofmann from a derivative of rye grass fungus (ergot), at the Swiss headquarters of Sandoz in 1938. Five years later, on April 19, 1943, he ingested 250 micrograms of LSD—the first LSD trip. He discovered its mind-bending properties during an epic bike ride home (April 19 is now celebrated annually as Bicycle Day). Hofmann not only survived the ride, but he continued as a chemist at Sandoz for many years. He lived to be a 102, dying in 2008. In an interview before his one hundredth birthday, Hofmann said LSD was "medicine for the soul."

PSYCHEDELICS

Psychedelic, from the Greek words *psyche* and *delos,* literally means "mind manifesting." Leary's own experience would convince him that LSD held potential for scientific discovery far beyond that of psilocybin.

At first Leary resisted the idea of including LSD in the Harvard Psilocybin Project—researching psilocybin was pushing administrators far enough. Another issue was the reputation LSD had of being a mind-control drug, researched by the military. In *High Priest,* Leary said, "Everything I had heard about lysergic acid sounded ominous to me. The mushrooms and peyote had grown naturally in the ground and had been used for thousands of years in wise Indian cultures. LSD, on the other hand, was a laboratory product and had quickly fallen into the hands of doctors and psychiatrists. Then, too, I was scared. . . . It was obvious that the more powerful LSD swept you far beyond the tender wisdom

January 24, 1962

Mr. William Wilson
c/o Helen Winn
597 Bedford Road
Pleasantville, New York

Dear Mr. Wilson:

Dr. Leary asked me to send you the enclosed psilocybin pills. They are different from the old pills in dosage, each of these pills is 10 mg. which is equal to 5 of the old ones. You might take two tablets for standard session, one for a mild experience and three or four for a deeper experience.

Sincerely,

Pearl Chan, Secretary
to Timothy Leary

pc

TOP AND ABOVE: Bicycle Day, animation by Centro Sperimentale di Cinematografia **RIGHT:** Letter to participant in the Harvard Psilocybin Project.

LIKE EVERYONE ELSE, I WAS BOTH FASCINATED AND FRIGHTENED BY THE LYSERGIC LORE.

of psilocybin. Like everyone else, I was both fascinated and frightened by the lysergic lore."

In November 1961, Tim was visited by Michael Hollingshead, an Englishman who had experimented with LSD and had bought a large supply of it from Sandoz. Neither Tim nor Dick had tried LSD, although they knew Huxley, Ginsberg, and Watts all had. And they had heard from Bill Wilson, the cofounder of Alcoholics Anonymous, who said LSD had stopped his drinking. While Michael was staying at Tim's house, he offered Tim, Maynard and Flo Ferguson, and George Litwin a taste of the LSD brew he had concocted.

After that first spoonful of LSD kicked in, Timothy (as he says in *High Priest*) was "tumbling and spinning, down the soft fibrous avenues to some central point which was just light. Just light, but not just light. It was the center of life. A burning, dazzling, throbbing, radiant core, pure pulsing, exulting light. An endless flame that contained everything—sound, touch, cell, seed, sense, soul, sleep, glory, glorifying, God, the hard eye of God. Merged with this pulsing flame it was possible to look out and see and participate in the entire cosmic drama."

Leary sobbed, overcome by the feeling that he had died and been reborn. He didn't speak for days. When he could speak, he said, "It was the most shattering experience of my life."

MERGED WITH THIS PULSING FLAME
IT WAS POSSIBLE TO LOOK OUT AND
SEE AND PARTICIPATE IN THE ENTIRE
COSMIC DRAMA.

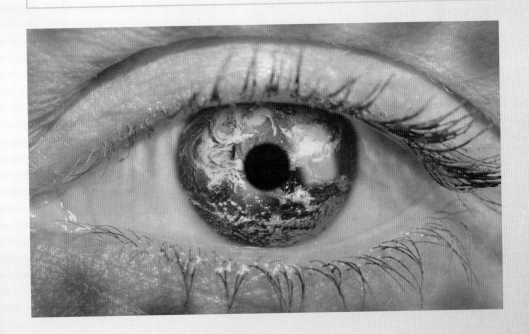

ABOVE: Photograph of Tim by Don Snyder. OPPOSITE: Photograph of Tim by Lawrence Schiller.

Leary noted Alpert's reaction: "Dick Alpert in particular was concerned. He could sense that we had moved beyond the game of psychology . . . From the date of this session it was inevitable that we would leave Harvard, that we would leave American society, and that we would spend the rest of our lives as mutants, faithfully following the instructions of our internal blueprints, and tenderly, gently, disregarding the parochial social insanities."

RAM DASS: *When Tim first took LSD, he didn't talk for about five days. He didn't talk to me or any of us. And I got afraid we'd lost Timothy. So, as a good lieutenant on the ship, I sort of battened down the hatches and told everybody not to touch the stuff and just to wait. When Timothy finally was able to speak, it was more like wow or phew or yes. And then we all started taking it.*

After that, it was as if all the LSD did was accentuate the direction Tim's life was going in, which was that of freeing himself from systems, freeing himself from that acculturation of the mind.

RAM DASS: *What he did was take leaps in seeing not only through the acculturation, but also through the whole identity as a human being, all of the ways that our mind creates our definition of reality. And he now had a much broader context from which to perceive the whole thing.*

LEARY SOBBED, OVERCOME
BY THE FEELING THAT
HE HAD DIED AND BEEN
REBORN. HE DIDN'T SPEAK
FOR DAYS. WHEN HE COULD
SPEAK, HE SAID, "IT WAS
THE MOST SHATTERING
EXPERIENCE OF MY LIFE."

TOP: *Leap* painting by Jon Marro. **ABOVE**: The car built to travel on railroad tracks.

When Alpert finally decided to try the stuff, he realized (as he related in *Being Ram Dass*) "that all this time in previous psychedelic sessions, I had been screwing around in the astral plane. LSD went beyond the astral, beyond form. It took you deeper, stripping away more of the layers of mind, and it lasted much longer. The peak of a trip carried you into a nova of consciousness and pure energy. Psilocybin had opened my spiritual heart. Now LSD opened the recesses of my mind and connected me to the very source of cosmic energy. No wonder Tim hadn't been able to speak."

LSD turned the Harvard Psilocybin Project into the Harvard Psychedelic Research Project.

RAM DASS: *Driving up to Sandoz in New Jersey in the huge black railroad limousine that I had from my father's railroad, with railroad wheels on the end of it, and Timothy and I are driving up to buy up this huge amount of LSD as Harvard professors.*

Mythic heroes travel unknown oceans in search of adventure and new lands. American astronauts were about to launch themselves into outer space. The psychedelic explorers were on a mythic adventure of their own.

RAM DASS: *Adventuring, playing with form, is such a deep wisdom teacher. Of all the qualities in Tim's and my relationship, adventuring was the dominant mythic one that we had. Adventurers. That's the word Timothy and I always used—we were adventurers. I often imagined we were on the African Queen and Timothy was the captain, sort of drunk, and I was the loyal Winston Churchill, except dull. I was standing right behind him—and that was an important role. It was the image I had of our relationship for a long time.*

ABOVE: Lama Tsultrim Allione.

ANDREW WEIL: *It is normal and natural to seek altered states of consciousness, high states; we do it all the time in various ways. Drugs are one way of getting into them. I think they made me aware of the magic in the world, of seeing things not just from the scientific perspective. They really connected me with nature in a way that I wasn't before. They showed me the potential of how changing things in here changes things out there. And that's been a major theme of my work.*

There are two classes of psychedelics: mescaline and its relatives—they're more stimulants than the ones called indoles, which are LSD and psilicybin and DMT, which really are remarkably light in their effects on the physical body. I think as a group these drugs are very nontoxic. The main dangers are psychological ones of people becoming panicked, terrified . . . but I think the positive potentials are terrific.

LAMA TSULTRIM ALLIONE: *From the beginning, Timothy Leary and Ram Dass (at that time Richard Alpert) were almost mythical characters in my life. I was beginning college, and the psychedelic revolution was happening. It was 1965, and I was introduced to LSD and a friend told me about the psychedelic experiments and about Leary and Alpert—these amazing people who were doing this very cutting-edge experimentation with consciousness. Everyone was so asleep and caught in this sort of postwar materialism, and it felt very dead and disconnected from nature. It was almost as though something strong and undeniable had to come into the consciousness of humanity to break that open and to create this change.*

The experiences that I had personally with psychedelics were all about opening my mind. Psychedelic means mind expansion, and it did that. It affected a whole generation of people that way. I mean, it ended the 1950s. And it was always for me about the spiritual journey. It's important to understand that certain drugs really are sacred substances. If you are going to use some of the sacred drugs,

TOP: Martin Luther King, Jr. **CENTER:** Janis Joplin. Photo by Don Snyder. **ABOVE:** Shaman in Tulum, Mexico.

ABOVE: Huichol yarn painting by Mariano Valadez Navarro.

use them in the right context with the right people. Timothy Leary and Richard Alpert recognized this. They blew open this world, this psychedelic world.

ROSHI JOAN HALIFAX: *It was as though the splitting of the atom was going to be followed by another kind of splitting, but it was the breaking open of the heart and the opening of the mind.*

JOHN PERRY BARLOW: *It's hard to describe what it was like taking LSD under the set and setting of the early '60s. The rending away from all of these intense paradigms of authority and monotheism, and culture. It was all up for grabs. It's hard to describe what that felt like.*

ROSHI JOAN HALIFAX: *Ram Dass was one of the main people in the 1960s who gave us all permission to push the edge. Tim, the same. We had permission calling to us because of the civil rights movement and the anti-war movement. The war in Vietnam was horrendous to many of us. We didn't understand it. It didn't make any sense to us. I mean, whose war is this? So to have iconic individuals in the '60s stand up and step off the map, it was fabulous.*

In the 1960s, Leary and Alpert dedicated themselves to exploring the vast reaches of inner space. They averaged one LSD session per week and took heroic doses. They saw themselves as psychedelic adventurers, exploring the nature of reality, encountering both the heaven and hell realms. They openly shared the results of their work, encouraging others to join them. LSD was at that time still fully legal. Leary and Alpert saw their

PSILOCYBIN HAD OPENED MY SPIRITUAL HEART. NOW LSD OPENED THE RECESSES OF MY MIND AND CONNECTED ME TO THE VERY SOURCE OF COSMIC ENERGY. NO WONDER TIM HADN'T BEEN ABLE TO SPEAK.

ABOVE: Tim with son Jack in Mexico.

research as connected to the centuries-long use of psychotropic plants by Indigenous peoples throughout the world.

> **TIMOTHY LEARY:** *The psychotropic drugs, which are not really recognized as existing, or valid tools, were demonized and glorified for the wrong reasons in the '60s. That's natural. The thing is, know what you're doing. LSD is not a drug like alcohol or barbiturates. LSD is a chemical that contains several hundred Encyclopedia Britannicas.*
>
> *So when you talk to someone who's taken LSD or if you've ever seen anyone who's taken LSD, his consciousness is being spun through many, many different levels of language, which are not the language of English, or French, or of Latin, but chemical languages of cell and nervous system, sense organs, which are many millions of years old. What's the reaction to taking LSD? If the person is unprepared and he swallows this local library of chemical messages, he's confused. He can be entranced and delighted, or he can be frightened.*

When the spring semester at Harvard ended, the Harvard Psychedelic Research Project held a summer session in Zihuatanejo, Mexico—a fishing village on the Pacific Ocean, a lovely set and setting. They were joined by Peggy Hitchcock, a trust-fund baby, who was thrilled to be part of Harvard research, along with around thirty-five professors, grad students, friends, and spouses of the project. Ram Dass called it a "psychedelic ashram"—a tribe of explorers and adventurers, all seekers of truth.

FIRED!

WHEN THEY returned to Cambridge from Mexico for the fall 1962 semester, all the psychedelic explorers in the project decided to live together so they could continue their explorations. Tim and Dick were teaching, keeping up with the Concord Prison Experiment, and experimenting at home. But the university higher-ups were beginning to distrust the project and formed a committee to oversee their work, as well as taking control of holding the substances they were using.

**DRUGS TESTED BY C.I.A.
ON MENTAL PATIENTS**

Documents Disclose Use in '58 of
LSD in Canadian Hospital

WASHINGTON, Aug. 2 – Mental patients at a Canadian hospital were given powerful tranquilizers and LSD in a 1958 experiment supported by a foundation that secretely dispensed money for the Central Inteligence Agency, medical financing records disclosed today.

The disclosure became one more element in a growing picture of the C.I.A.'s 25-year attempt to learn how to control the human mind.

Eventually Leary decided the university was hampering their work, so they broke from the Department of Social Relations at Harvard and created a nonprofit, the International Federation for Internal Freedom (IFIF), to support their work with psychedelics. But there were a lot of reports around campus about students taking these drugs. After all, the students could score their own LSD or mescaline. The newspapers caught wind of the story, and Leary and Alpert were admonished on the front page of the *New York Times*. The FDA opened an investigation into illegal drug sales in Cambridge.

At one point, Dave McClelland called a meeting with clinical students and faculty of the Psychology Department to talk about the Harvard Psychedelic Research Project. Herb Kelman, one of the research scientists who had been part of the secret CIA mind-control experiments with LSD ten years previously (they were trying to find a way the drug could be used in warfare), and who had not ever taken LSD himself, said the project should be restructured or terminated.

News of the clash within the department appeared in the student newspaper, the *Harvard Crimson,* and was picked up by Boston newspapers. A misleading headline in the *Boston Herald* read "Hallucination Drug Fought at Harvard—350 Students Take Pills." Leary and Alpert had indeed given psilocybin to many *subjects,* but they were not all *students* by any means. Turning *subjects* into *students* turned two Harvard

professors into leaders of a campus drug ring.

Ever the scientists, Leary and Alpert published articles in journals and delivered papers at conferences. The word was out—and their program was becoming popular. Maybe too popular! The dean of Harvard, John Monro, warned undergraduates about the mind-distorting drug, which the papers picked up on again. Monro blamed "over-enthusiastic scientific experimenters" and "private psilocybin parties" for promoting drugs on campus.

HUSTON SMITH: *Psilocybin was to be given only to graduate students, but there was one slip.*

RAM DASS: *That guy that I turned on, one person, was somebody to whom I was attracted. It's interesting about feeling like the outcast. I would never have turned on an undergraduate except for my homosexuality. When I was brought into the president of Harvard's office to be fired, I guess I felt like an outcast because, by his game rules, I was playing outside the box, and it opened my whole life to a life that is better than I ever would have expected.*

PEGGY HITCHCOCK: *I think someone wrote an article in the Harvard Crimson talking about this. And the parents of this one boy found out about it and they went to the officials at Harvard and said, What's going on here?*

That winter was when Richard and Tim were thrown out of Harvard. They had already started the experiment with psychedelics in the prison system, at Concord Prison. This was a bit of a shock to Richard, to put it mildly, who had been on the tenure track and had his career all mapped out. The irony was that one would have expected that Tim would be the one who would be asked to leave. Of course, they didn't renew Tim's contract. Even though the work that they were doing in the prison system was very valuable, it was clear that they were putting the university in a very untenable position, or at least that's what the university thought.

And so Richard Alpert, who was happy and proud to be a Harvard professor, was dismissed from Harvard for giving LSD to an undergraduate. Leary's appointment to Harvard was coming to a close and would not be renewed, yet he was let go for failing to show up for classes. It didn't matter to him; Leary was off in Mexico setting up a training center for psychedelic research at the Hotel Catalina in Zihuatanejo, Mexico.

TIMOTHY LEARY: *You were on the tenure track.*

RAM DASS: *I know I was. And you laughed. You laughed.*

TIMOTHY LEARY: *If it weren't for me, you'd be a . . .*

RAM DASS: *I'd be somebody today.*

TIMOTHY LEARY: *. . . retired Harvard professor.*

RAM DASS: *You blew my cover. You blew me apart.*

TIMOTHY LEARY: *I know it.*

RAM DASS: *I would have been set today.*

TIMOTHY LEARY: *I ruined your academic career.*

RAM DASS: *You did. You absolutely did.*

TIMOTHY LEARY: *There's a joke about that. On an interview they said I ruined an entire generation. I'm like, oh, that's seventy-two million people. They said, Don't you feel any regret? And I said, "One thing I feel is that only a hundred thousand of them had the decency to thank me."*

ANDREW WEIL: *I had joined the editorial board of the Harvard Crimson, the Harvard newspaper, and there were stories beginning to go around about the drug experiments with Leary and Alpert. I was majoring in botany and my mentor was Richard Evans Schultes, the head of the Harvard University Herbaria and] Botanical Museum, who was one of the great experts on psychoactive plants.*

There were very few people at the Crimson who had any scientific background, so it was logical that I became the reporter who dealt with the psychedelic issue. In 1962, things started to heat up around what was going on at Harvard. I became the investigative reporter covering the Leary/Alpert story, and I ended up playing a key role in getting information that led to Alpert's being fired in 1963. Leary was never fired. He used to say he had been fired from Harvard, but he hadn't. That story was front page news in the New York Times, probably the first time most Americans had ever heard of psychedelic drugs like LSD or mushrooms, so I do think that that whole episode is what exploded this [use of

LSD] out of Harvard into the nation and the culture. I was in a very difficult role. For one thing, I had taken these drugs and had positive feelings for them, but I had to do life as a straight undergraduate who was doing this investigative reporting.

I don't have remorse. I think things happened in the only way things could have been. He wouldn't have been Ram Dass if he hadn't been fired from Harvard. I wouldn't be who I am. This was some karmic interaction and it played out the way it was supposed to.

ZACH LEARY: *Within popular culture it was a Pandora's box. You know, the second youth culture got hold of LSD, it exploded, much greater than anybody knew it would, much greater than Tim knew it would.*

ANDREW WEIL: *I think Tim was especially naïve; he had an innocence about him, which I don't think Dick had. Tim really did not anticipate the kind of reaction he received. At the same time, he had a great propensity to say things that really pushed people's buttons, and he enjoyed that. He loved to say that LSD was the greatest aphrodisiac in the world, for example. Or turn on, tune in, drop out. As he got older, I saw him get angrier, and towards the end of his life, when he got up in front of audiences, there was a lot of anger that came out as well. I think he was drinking quite a bit in that period, so I'm sure it was associated with that as well.*

TIMOTHY LEARY: *If groups take LSD together, it's a bond, and that's what happened at Harvard. We bonded up. And Kelman, this professor that got you thrown out. He's very brilliant but a very uptight guy. He was right, because in our department, the research . . .*

RAM DASS: *. . . the Social Relations Department or Center for Research in Personality. 5 Divinity Avenue.*

TIMOTHY LEARY: *Yeah, right. The hot shots before we were there. When we started our research, out of twenty new graduate students, eighteen signed up for ours.*

RAM DASS: *They wanted to be with us, and that's why we were turned on.*

TIMOTHY LEARY: *That's why we were fired. Not for drugs.*

RAM DASS: *No, we took all the graduate students away from the other faculty.*

TIMOTHY LEARY: *Yeah, and that's the worst sin.*

RAM DASS: *Exactly. We were more interesting than they were.*

RALPH METZNER: *It ended up so many of the graduate students wanted to work with Leary and almost all the other professors lost students, assistants, you see, which pissed them off, of course.*

I DON'T HAVE REMORSE. I THINK THINGS HAPPENED IN THE ONLY WAY THINGS COULD HAVE BEEN. HE WOULDN'T HAVE BEEN RAM DASS IF HE HADN'T BEEN FIRED FROM HARVARD. I WOULDN'T BE WHO I AM. THIS WAS SOME KARMIC INTERACTION AND IT PLAYED OUT THE WAY IT WAS SUPPOSED TO.

Leary and Alpert desperately wanted to continue their work, which was becoming highly controversial, but was still legal. Where could they go? IFIF tried to set up a psychedelic retreat in Mexico, but it backfired and they were kicked out. They were also kicked out of Dominica and Antigua. Then Peggy Hitchcock said her brothers had just come into their inheritance from the Mellon family and had a big estate—a property of 2,500 acres and a huge mansion—that they weren't using.

TOP: Alan Ginsberg, Peggy Mellon Hitchcock, Tim Leary. **ABOVE**: Zach Leary.

MILLBROOK
(1963–1968)

PEGGY HITCHCOCK: *Just by chance my brothers inherited quite a bit of money and they had decided to use this money to buy this huge property in Millbrook, New York, as a good investment. On the property was the original house that had belonged to the person who developed the property back in the late nineteenth, early twentieth century. It kind of wanted to be haunted. It was huge, with lots of turrets and curved glass. It was really beautiful. I talked to my brothers. They weren't going to use it, and they said sure, we'll rent you the house for a dollar a year.*

ABOVE: The "castle" at Millbrook.

It was perfect. With Tim's children, Susan and Jack, and a hodgepodge of friends and acquaintances, they launched into communal living. Millbrook was paradise, with meadows, pine forests, fields of corn and sunflowers, a lake and waterfall, a creek with stone bridges, apple orchards, livestock, and horse stables. A second house on the property had a bowling alley, and another residence had a swimming pool. The main house, known as the Castle, had over sixty rooms, ten bathrooms, and a library. Ten people lived there full-time, and weekends were party time, with at least half a dozen guests. Nearby was an experimental art collective (USCO), cofounded by the psychedelic artist Steve Durkee, who had married Dick's friend Barbara Greer (in 1967, Steve and Barbara, along with Jonathan Altman, founded the interreligious Lama Foundation in New Mexico). The art collective included Stewart Brand, who later started the *Whole Earth Catalog*. Barbara brought the group together with the Millbrook crowd.

At Millbrook, Tim and Dick continued their research and designed new experiments. Tim kept records of all the sessions. They taught weekend workshops—seminars (without

O NOBLY BORN, O YOU OF GLORIOUS ORIGINS, REMEMBER YOUR RADIANT TRUE NATURE, THE ESSENCE OF MIND. TRUST IT. RETURN TO IT. IT IS HOME.

—*THE TIBETAN BOOK OF THE DEAD*

TOP: Jack, Tim, and Susan in Italy. **ABOVE**: Richard Alpert, Timothy Leary, and Ralph Metzner.

giving psychedelics) to give people the tools for a good acid trip: how to run a session, how to create set and setting, and other aspects of the spiritual journey, like meditation, Gurdjieff exercises, hatha yoga, and tantra. And they continued working on their rewrite of *The Tibetan Book of the Dead* as well as a journal called the *Psychedelic Review*.

Aldous Huxley had introduced them to *The Tibetan Book of the Dead,* translated by Walter Evans-Wentz. The text is used by Tibetan Buddhists as a guide for dying and going through the bardo between death and the next rebirth. It was almost identical to the ego death on psychedelics. It turned out that the maps Leary and Alpert and the other psychedelic astronauts were seeking already existed.

Tim and Ralph Metzner started rewriting *The Tibetan Book of the Dead* into a psychedelic manual. Ram Dass was busy running the Millbrook community, but helped with trip descriptions, ideas, and theories. Tim, Ralph, and Richard put all their energy into finishing *The Psychedelic Experience: A Manual Based on the Tibetan Book of the Dead,* dedicated to Aldous Huxley. Alan Watts read a draft and was delighted by their exploration of the various states of consciousness. It sold quickly, their first best-selling book. It made them realize that even though they were no longer at the heights of academia, they were at the cutting edge of a major paradigm shift in American culture.

In an effort to raise money to keep their inner explorations and research going, they rebranded IFIF as the Castalia Foundation (based on Hermann Hesse's book *The Glass Bead Game,* in which a community of seekers live in a place called Castalia).

TIMOTHY LEARY: *There's a deep fear that all cultures put into people about dying. I am openly enjoying the prospect of dying, which I got from* The Tibetan Book of the Dead, *by the way. That was our first bestseller.*

RAM DASS: *Isn't it interesting that the first bestseller was* The Tibetan Book of the Dead, *and here you are, and the dying thing is your next bestseller. You've had a lot of bestsellers, but this is the major bestseller at the moment.*

TIMOTHY LEARY: *Well, we walk it, not just talk it.*

RAM DASS: *What's the relation between* The Tibetan Book of the Dead *and the way you're seeing death now?*

TIMOTHY LEARY: *Basically, it tells you that the stages before your so-called death are the most important times of your life. And if you do it right, you'll see the white light before you croak.*

RAM DASS: *Before you croak?*

TIMOTHY LEARY: *Die. Check out. I'm deliberately using these terms.*

RAM DASS: *You don't think it's for the forty-nine days after death?*

ABOVE: Ken Kesey in center. Neal Cassidy on right. **OPPOSITE**: Painting of Maria Sabina by Martin Bridge.

TIMOTHY LEARY: *Everybody gets the Timothy Leary they deserve. Everybody gets the Ram Dass, and everybody gets* The Tibetan Book of the Dead . . .

RAM DASS: . . . *they deserve.*

TIMOTHY LEARY: *My* Tibetan Book of the Dead *shows you how to die up to the moment of death.*

RAM DASS: *Is it impacting your preparations for your own death?*

TIMOTHY LEARY: *Well, it prepared me for it.*

RAM DASS: *Is it relevant now?*

TIMOTHY LEARY: *Haven't read it.*

RAM DASS: *I haven't read it for twenty years.*

PEGGY HITCHCOCK: *We used to use* The Tibetan Book of the Dead *as a manual for psychedelic trips. It is a manual of leaving your body and going into what they call a bardo state, so it's really a manual for death. How you relate that experience to your own death is another question. It's all very well and good to say it's a model, but yet it's not really, because you know the real thing can be a different story.*

LAMA TSULTRIM ALLIONE: *What Leary and Ram Dass saw right in the beginning with LSD was very important, which is that it's connected to the bardo, it's connected to the time after death. Bardo means "in-between"; bar do, the in-between state. This is a bardo, too. We are in the bardo of life right now. Then there's the bardo of dream. Usually we think of the bardo between death and rebirth, but that's just* *one of the six different bardos. They were talking about the bardo connected to* The Tibetan Book of the Dead, *the bardo between death and rebirth. They identified LSD as a vehicle to pre-experience what that would be like. I think that reading* The Psychedelic Experience *was a thread that led me to Tibetan Buddhism.*

In the summer of 1964, Ken Kesey had already published his novel *One Flew Over the Cuckoo's Nest,* which was based on his experience working in a mental hospital while taking part in the CIA-funded research project on LSD. That July, he and his Merry Pranksters were on a cross-country trip in *Furthur,* their rainbow-painted bus, and honked down the driveway to Millbrook, loudspeakers blaring, unannounced, and at a bad time. They were ready to party, but the Millbrook gang was tired, having just come down from a trip.

Later, Kesey and the Merry Pranksters held Acid Tests, in which they gave LSD to hundreds of partygoers, much to the dismay of the scientists at Millbrook. At the time, Tim considered LSD a sacrament, not to be used as a party drug. Tim had spent a considerable amount of time at a Vedic ashram near Boston. Fred Swain, a World War II air force major who had become a Vedanta Hindu monk called Sri Kalidas, lived there. (Fred had had a mushroom trip with María Sabina, a Mazatec *curandera,* shaman, and poet, in the mountains of Oaxaca.) Tim was thrilled to be able to share psychedelic experiences and the company of those who had renounced the world in order to pursue the visionary quest.

Alpert was also attracted to Eastern concepts, which they all felt were where the answers lay to their quest. Hermann Hesse's books (*Siddhartha, The Glass Bead Game, Demian*), the *Tao Te Ching,* the Bhagavad Gita, and P. D. Ouspensky's *In Search of the Miraculous* made a journey to the East sound very inviting. Allen Ginsberg had gone to India, met the Dalai Lama, and discussed consciousness with Swami Sivananda. When he returned and showed up in Millbrook, they could sense his newfound spiritual energy. Then Ralph was invited to go to India to consult with Hindu and Buddhist teachers about

IT MADE THEM
REALIZE THAT
EVEN THOUGH
THEY WERE NO
LONGER AT THE
HEIGHTS OF
ACADEMIA, THEY
WERE AT THE
CUTTING EDGE
OF A MAJOR
PARADIGM SHIFT
IN AMERICAN
CULTURE.

psychedelics. Meanwhile, Tim and Dick were becoming popular speakers and were busy lecturing to big crowds.

Over four years of communal living at Millbrook and scores of shared psilocybin and LSD sessions, Leary and Alpert developed a close and trusting relationship. Richard was the mother, baking bread, taking care of the domestic scene, and basically raising Tim's children.

RAM DASS: *I got into the really conscious thing in my mind that I could justify my life being a support system for Timothy's vision to find expression. It meant raising money; it meant raising children; it meant cooking; it meant getting housing; it meant moving jeeps and stuff to islands we were being thrown off of. You know, it was incredible. It meant setting up foundations. It was all the public relations stuff to try to keep the game from getting out of hand.*

My capacity to be in that relationship to Timothy, part of it I'm sure, arises from the fact that I'm basically gay. My relationship with Timothy was never physical love, but there was a love affair going on. I mean we loved each other. We really loved each other and I became very trustworthy for Tim to push against, to lean on in a way to get further out, and Timothy was taking me out with him.

COMING TOGETHER AND FALLING APART

AT MILLBROOK, they took LSD once a week in programmed sessions. Meanwhile, on the West Coast, Aldous Huxley was dying of cancer. He asked Tim to guide him in an LSD session using *The Psychedelic Experience.* Tim told him it would be better to have Aldous's wife, Laura, guide him. In *Flashbacks,* Leary said Aldous's final words to him were, "Be gentle with them, Timothy. They want to be free, but they don't know how. Teach them. Reassure them." At his request, Laura gave her husband LSD as

ABOVE: Leary with Laura Huxley.

he drew in his final breaths and told him to concentrate on the light. Aldous Huxley died on November 22, 1963, the same day that President John F. Kennedy was assassinated. It felt like a profound synchronicity.

> **JOHN PERRY BARLOW:** *I'd been hearing out on the West Coast they'd been filling bathtubs full of LSD, feeding it to anyone that wanted to come in and drink as much as they wanted, and playing crazy music for them. I thought, this is fucking drug abuse.*

Peggy Hitchcock, with whom Leary had an on-again, off-again relationship, introduced him to Nena von Schlebrügge, a beautiful blonde fashion model, and they fell in love.

They were married at Grace Church in the nearby town. Dick was the best man. Tim's daughter, Susan, was one of the bridesmaids.

> **RAM DASS:** *I remember your wedding. I was the best man.*

> **TIMOTHY LEARY:** *You were the best man. Of course you were.*

> **RAM DASS:** *Yeah, of course I remember. Who am I to you? A projection?*

ABOVE: John Perry Barlow. **LEFT:** Nena von Schlebrügge.

TIMOTHY LEARY: *Well, you are a . . . We're not like soulmates. Good friends and long-term friends and mutual teaching.*

PRIEST: *Remember as much of the vows as you can, and "I will."*

Charles Mingus played piano and Maynard Ferguson jammed with Miles Davis's sidemen, entertaining the 150 guests who were high on LSD, grass, and mushrooms. The punch at the reception was spiked with LSD.

ROSHI JOAN HALIFAX: *I would have loved to have been in the room when Tim and Nena were married. I mean, he was such a trickster, and she was a total fierce sort of jade dragon. She's brilliant, phenomenally beautiful, and they must have had one heck of a time. I cannot imagine. You put Tim Leary and Nena in the same room with LSD, oh my goodness. Ram Dass was in the mix somewhere. Who knows who was in love with whom in the whole situation. I've heard various stories and versions. The people who were magnetized into Millbrook at that time and into that world briefly had a king and queen bee, Tim and Nena. Must have been interesting.*

Tim and Nena took off on a honeymoon trip to India, leaving Tim's children in the care of Alpert. After tripping through Japan, they headed to India, where Ralph Metzner was living at Crank's Ridge, a bohemian colony near Almora in the foothills of the Himalayas (called "Holy Man's Ridge" by the hippies). It was home to Lama Anagarika Govinda (author of *The Way of the White Clouds*) and his wife, Li Gotami. The German-born Tibetan Buddhist's ashram was a must-visit for spiritual seekers, from Allen Ginsberg and Gary Snyder to R. D. Laing and Tibetologist Robert Thurman (who in a few years would marry Nena and have four children; their daughter, Uma Thurman, is a well-known actress). Tim and Nena settled in.

In an amazing almost encounter that started on a local bus, Tim became fascinated with Hari Das Baba, a silent *saddhu* (who later would become Richard Alpert's teacher). Tim followed him off the bus, but when the driver blew his horn to get going, Tim got back on the bus. Had he continued to follow Hari Das for five more minutes, Tim would have met Neem Karoli Baba, the Indian saint known to his followers as Maharajji, who became Alpert's guru and changed his whole life.

TIMOTHY LEARY: *Of all the Americans that went around on that holy trip in India, you and I, because we had a lot of acid, were more open to it . . .*

RAM DASS: *Yes, absolutely.*

TIMOTHY LEARY: *. . . than 90 percent. It's no accident that we totally know about it, but we did the same thing. If I'd gotten off the bus, I wouldn't have gone back to Millbrook, right? Did you go to India before me?*

TOP TO BOTTOM: From D.A. Pennebaker's film of Tim and Nena's wedding.

BE GENTLE WITH THEM, TIMOTHY.
THEY WANT TO BE FREE, BUT THEY
DON'T KNOW HOW. TEACH THEM.
REASSURE THEM.

—ALDOUS HUXLEY

TOP: Maynard Ferguson. **ABOVE**: Leary on roof at Millbrook.

ABOVE AND RIGHT: Nena and Tim on honeymoon in India.

RAM DASS: *No, after. Two years later.*

TIMOTHY LEARY: *That's right.*

RAM DASS: *With David Padwa.*

TIMOTHY LEARY: *Yeah, oh, God.*

RAM DASS: *And then Nepal, and then came back down and then was in a car that met this guy [Maharajji] on the same road you were on.*

TIMOTHY LEARY: *Yeah. Because I remember when Allen [Ginsberg] came back from India and we all wanted to go, and I went before you.*

RAM DASS: *You and Allen Ginsberg went first.*

Together with Metzner, Tim and Nena visited Sri Krishna Prem. Metzner felt that Govinda was a scholar, whereas Krishna Prem felt like a real sage. Tim called Krishna Prem "the wisest man in India," and followed his advice to return to the West. When they left India, Tim and Nena's marriage was essentially over.

PEGGY HITCHCOCK: *In his life there was a big disconnect between his heart and his mind. And his mind was completely in charge always, and the heart kind of got left behind.*

ABOVE: Susan Homer, Richard, Tim, and Peggy Hitchcock

RAM DASS: *Intimacy. They wanted psychological intimacy. He was offering a different kind of intimacy, which is the kind of intimacy he and I had, which is the intimacy of shared awareness. He didn't get as deep into psychodynamic stuff. I mean, here he was a psychologist who had created a very, very highly regarded diagnostic psychological inventory for assessing personality. The reason he was so good at that is 'cause he was outside of that. That domain, or that plane of consciousness, didn't engage him, so that most of the women around him were always disappointed.*

Ralph Metzner had come back to Millbrook before Tim and Nena and was shocked at what he found. Paradise had devolved into hell. People were high all the time, day and night. Dick was focused on getting as high as possible. He and five others had locked themselves in the meditation room and ingested 400 micrograms of LSD every four hours, for two weeks; Alpert realized they were staying at a very high plateau but couldn't get any higher. Dirty dishes piled up in the sink. A Tibetan monkey was now part of the menagerie. The cars were broken, the furnace blew up, and they were $50,000 in debt.

Tim and Nena returned in the early spring, but Tim was in no shape to handle what was going on at Millbrook; he was having a hard time with his marriage. In the process of fighting and breaking up with Nena, he and Dick broke up as well. He blamed Alpert's irresponsibility for allowing the group to fall into such discord. Tim thought Dick

ABOVE: Photo of Richard by Carl Studna.

had strayed from their mission and instead had created a drug commune. There were two basic camps at Millbrook: those like Dick who wanted to explore high states of consciousness and those who wanted a sense of order.

RAM DASS: *It wasn't all fun and games. I mean it was extremely scary because I had grown up in a family that treasured antiques, for example, so that my apartment in Cambridge when I was a Harvard professor was full of absolute beautiful antiques, and then I moved to Millbrook where it was monkeys and aardvarks and cats and six dogs and many children. We were in a sixty-three-room house, you know? And I watched my antiques one by one be destroyed before my eyes. I didn't have the intelligence to just sell them.*

It was undercutting something very deep in me.

Then as the years went on something very profound happened because I started to distinguish between visionary and revolutionary, and Timothy was both. I loved

THE AWAKENINGS
THAT PSYCHEDELICS
PROVIDED HIM
NEVER LASTED
LONG. ALPERT
HUNGERED FOR A
WAY TO MAINTAIN
AND INTEGRATE
EXPANDED STATES
OF CONSCIOUSNESS.

the visionary part. The revolutionary part didn't resonate with me. I'm more of an evolutionary than a revolutionary person. And what I saw was that the revolutionary part of Tim was costing so much psychically and financially and socially and everything. We're $50,000 in debt and no matter how hard I tried I couldn't pay it off and we were getting further and further out all the time. I thought as much fun as it was, now it was no longer so much fun, and the other part of it was being in a relationship with somebody that way, ultimately that other part of you never develops. I realized that I was a more creative person than the situation was allowing me to be. At that point, that's when we started to pull apart. We had a deep, deep friendship, but we also had a deep enmity.

ABOVE: Zuleikha Sufi whirling. Photo by Katie Johnson.

Alpert could now see the destructive side to Tim's game, and in June 1965 he went to Europe for the summer, where he lunched with Albert Hofmann and talked about LSD as a sacrament; Hofmann understood Dick's desire to "journey to the edge." When he returned, he was met at the train station by Leary and Metzner, who basically threw him out of Millbrook.

In the fall of 1965, Richard Alpert left Millbrook for good. The awakenings that psychedelics provided him never lasted long. Alpert hungered for a way to maintain and integrate expanded states of consciousness. Getting high and coming down again and again had created a sense of despair.

ROSHI JOAN HALIFAX: *You know, eventually the world of mind-manifesting substances became more like decoration. In this era of the civil rights and the anti-war movements, I realized that to be engaged politically, I had also to be engaged with my own mind. I just wanted to really train my mind to be very, very stable and to be able to perceive my own mental continuum clearly and not have it so decorated.*

TIMOTHY LEARY

LSD PROPHET TO PRISONER

THIRTY-YEAR-OLD Rosemary Woodruff visited Millbrook and spent the night with Tim. The next day, the two of them painted interlocking triangles on the huge red brick chimney of the mansion— the *maha yantra* symbol for sexual union. Rosemary was happy to dedicate herself to caring for Tim and his children, and she wanted to have his child. She reminded Tim of Marianne.

By 1965, all the original inhabitants of Millbrook had left. Alpert was touring with the Grateful Dead. Metzner was

ABOVE: Tim and Rosemary Woodruff. **OPPOSITE**: Photo of Tim by Don Snyder.

living in Rosemary's apartment in the city. It was just Leary, Rosemary, and Tim's son Jack. They were under constant police surveillance; the local district attorney was said to be planning a raid. Tim took the advance he received for his autobiography and headed to the Yucatan with Rosemary, Susan, and Jack for a month-long Christmas vacation.

Entering the Mexican border checkpoint in Laredo, Texas, in December, they were turned away. They swung the car around to return to America, and in what was probably a preplanned bust (wiretaps at Millbrook could have disclosed their itinerary), they were arrested for slightly over a third of an ounce of marijuana and three partially smoked joints. With bail set for a total of $25,000, they returned to Millbrook to fight the conviction. On February 7, 1966, Tim and Susan were indicted on three federal charges: smuggling marijuana, transporting marijuana, and failure to pay the federal marijuana tax (the Marihuana Tax Act of 1937). Tim decided to go to trial so he could challenge the laws that made smoking pot illegal. Despite their breakup, Alpert wired Tim.

To no one's surprise, the verdict came back guilty. For two of the counts, Tim was sentenced to twenty years in prison and a $20,000 fine, and for failure to pay the federal tax on marijuana, he was sentenced to an additional ten years in prison and a $10,000 fine.

ABOVE: Photo at Millbrook by Don Snyder. **LEFT**: Triangles painting by Tim and Rosemary on Millbrook. **BOTTOM**: Tim and Rosemary.

Susan, who had hidden the pot in her underwear while the bust was happening, was sent to a reformatory. The charges against Rosemary and Jack were dropped for lack of evidence against them.

TIMOTHY LEARY: *We're not going to solve this problem [of psychedelics] by putting leading scientists like myself in jail for thirty- or forty-year prison terms, for doing nothing more than trying to understand these new forms of energy. Yet, there's no evidence that we've done any damage to society or to ourselves or to other people.*

Money was problematic. The appeal could cost $100,000, especially since it would eventually reach up to the US Supreme Court. Alpert wrote a fundraising letter for the Timothy Leary Psychedelic Defense Fund, in which he stated: "He is in my estimation, the one person most responsible for introducing LSD (a consciousness-expanding chemical) into our culture as a folk sacrament rather than as a psychiatric tool for the study of psychosis. . . . Some of you might wish to consider this a Head Tax."

Tim knew it would take around three years for the case to go to the Supreme Court and the decision to come down, so he had time to pitch himself back into the revolution.

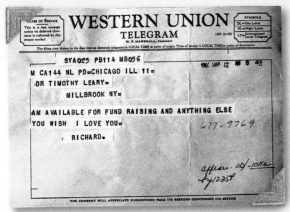

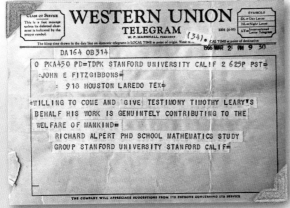

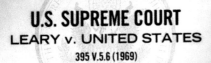

The trial had created a ton of publicity about LSD use in America, and Timothy Leary was ready to be a public figure. But before things could really get going, in April the big house at Millbrook was raided at 1 a.m. by the local sheriff and the assistant district attorney of Dutchess County, G. Gordon Liddy, a former FBI agent and the future Watergate felon. Leary and Liddy started what would turn into a running dialogue in the coming decades. Rosemary called the lawyers.

TOP LEFT: Telegrams in support of Tim.
TOP RIGHT: Photo of Tim by Lawrence Schiller.

> I RECOMMEND RESPECTFULLY TO THIS COMMITTEE THAT YOU
> CONSIDER LEGISLATION THAT WILL LICENSE RESPONSIBLE
> ADULTS TO USE THESE DRUGS FOR SERIOUS PURPOSES
> SUCH AS SPIRITUAL GROWTH, THE PURSUIT OF KNOWLEDGE,
> OR IN THEIR OWN PERSONAL DEVELOPMENT.

Rosemary was called to testify against Leary before the grand jury and refused on religious grounds. She was sentenced to and served a month in jail for contempt of court. She suspected Tim was having a good time in her absence.

The use of LSD had mushroomed in America and was at epidemic proportions. In May 1966, the congressional Subcommittee on Health and Scientific Research was examining the chemical's risks and therapeutic possibilities. Chairman Thomas Dodd, a conservative Democrat, had convened the subcommittee hearings to learn about recreational drug use among the youth in America. Even though he was a controversial figure, Leary was still a scientist as well as a proponent of LSD and was called to testify

TOP LEFT: Senator Edward Kennedy at hearing. TOP RIGHT: Dr. Leary testifying.

JOINT HEARING
BEFORE THE
SELECT COMMITTEE ON INTELLIGENCE
AND THE
SUBCOMMITTEE ON
HEALTH AND SCIENTIFIC RESEARCH
OF THE
COMMITTEE ON HUMAN RESOURCES
UNITED STATES SENATE
NINETY-FIFTH CONGRESS
FIRST SESSION

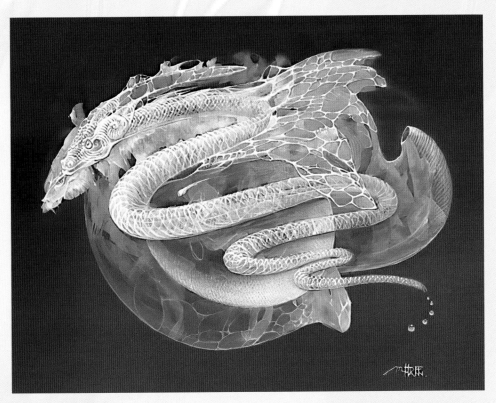

TOP: *Serpent Egg* by Martina Hoffman.

before Congress. Two Boston Irish Catholic families were about to meet: the Learys and the Kennedys.

In his congressional testimony, Tim said: "The use of psychedelic drugs such as marijuana, mescaline, and LSD is out of control in the United States today. I have never urged indiscriminate use of LSD and I've never propagandized for LSD. Strangely enough, my position on LSD is exactly that of the present Johnson administration: I believe that the present laws which penalize sale and manufacture of LSD are right.

We have been told today, and we read in the papers reports from sociologists that from between 15 to 50 percent and in some cases up to 65 and 70 percent of our college students are experimenting with these mind-opening chemicals. And I recommend respectfully to this committee that you consider legislation that will license responsible adults to use these drugs for serious purposes such as spiritual growth, the pursuit of knowledge, or in their own personal development. To obtain such a license, the applicant, I think, should have to meet physical, intellectual, and emotional criteria."

> **SENATOR EDWARD KENNEDY:** *Your testimony, I understand extremely clearly, and it's becoming more clear now, that you feel indiscriminant possession is something that you do not support.*

TURN ON, TUNE IN, DROP OUT.

LEFT: Campaign poster when Leary ran for governor of California.
ABOVE: Photo of Leary by Lisa Law.

TIMOTHY LEARY: *For six years, sir, I have been against indiscriminate use . . .*

KENNEDY: *. . . indiscriminate use, all right.*

TIMOTHY LEARY: *I have under my personal supervision witnessed over 3,000 ingestions of LSD.*

[OFF-CAMERA VOICE]: *3,000. Well, can you briefly describe the effects of it?*

TIMOTHY LEARY: *Oh . . . [chuckles] . . . Uh, no sir. You might say, every cell in my body began to dissolve, and to break down. I was afraid I'd become a puddle on the floor. Then I saw a huge serpent coming up. The serpent swallowed me; I went into the serpent's stomach and later I was excreted, and I exploded, and then, uh . . .*

ROSHI JOAN HALIFAX: *You see Teddy Kennedy there and it's like, oh my gosh, these guys must have been having their own little mental breakdown listening to him.*

TIMOTHY LEARY: *Now, by this time even the most experienced and hard-bitten psychologist is likely to be crouching under the table, saying in thirty years of practice I've never listened to anything so frightening and so far out.*

Now, actually, if you told this story to a Hindu, he'd say, "Oh yes, the third dream of Vishnu," or, "Oh yes, that's like the eleventh chapter of the Bhagavad Gita." Well, we also have neurological and atomical explanations for the so-called hallucinations of LSD. Hallucinations are not mysterious or supernatural; hallucinations are the nervous sytem having experiences for which we don't have words.

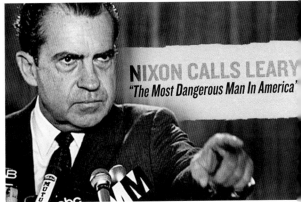

TOP: "Bed In for Peace" with John Lennon and Yoko Ono. Rosemary and Tim in front. Photo by Gerry Deiter.

JOANNA HARCOURT-SMITH: *He felt very strongly that he would be able to convince Congress that psychotropic drugs be given over to the medical profession for healing purposes. And he knew that the minute they decided to make this a law-enforcement issue it would be everywhere. There would be no stopping it. Everybody would be able to get hold of it. That was terrible for him. That's where he developed a very strong rebel side towards the government.*

Leary would be busted again in a few years for transportation of marijuana, not possession, and wind up in prison. Before that bust, however, came the Human Be-In in San Francisco's Golden Gate Park on January 14, 1967, the kickoff event to what would become the Summer of Love in Haight-Ashbury. It was here that Leary brought his famous phrase, "Turn on, tune in, drop out," to the public at large, and it turned him into the prophet of psychedelia. Gone was the social science researcher; Tim was at the center of the hippie movement.

LEARY GOES TO PRISON ON COAST

To Start Term of 1 to 10 Years

The first announced candidate for California governor in 1970 came to town Friday night and gave prospective voters a taste of his "politics of pleasure."

Dr. Timothy Leary, former Harvard psychology professor and a man who has continually challenged marijuana laws, said he is "floating" (not running) to Sacramento.

About 2,000 persons were in Cal Poly's Men's

MILDENHALL, England (UPI)—The homesick American sergeant drank glass after glass of Scotch and gland at everyone at the party who tried to talk to him. Finally he rose, unsteadily, knocked over a lamp and ran out the door.

LOS ANGELES (UPI) — Students Friday called for twoday strikes at all nine University of California campuses and at least two of the 19 state colleges to protest the use of police and National Guard troops to quell disturbances at the UC Berkeley campus.

The authorities

protesting the closure of a "Peoples Park" on the Berkeley campus. One demonstrator, a non-student, was fatally wounded by police during the protest last week.

Later, the guard was called in and a helicopter was used to

Berkeley Academic Senate met Friday night and condemned police actions near the campus.

The senate also voted to seek mutual de-escalation of the situation by calling for withdrawal of "massive police and military presence on the

It called for returning the park to those using it and condemned the use of the helicopter as "monstrous" aerial trespassing.

While students called for a two-day strike at all UC campuses Monday and Tues-

LEARY'S DISGUISE

CENTER LEFT: Leary's mugshot. **BOTTOM:** Eldridge Cleaver and Leary in Algeria. Photo © Associated Press.

ART LINKLETTER (WHO BLAMED LEARY FOR HIS DAUGHTER DIANE'S SUICIDE): *As that poisonous, evil man, Dr. Timothy Leary, has said [about acid], it is a way to "tune in, turn on, and drop out."*

TIMOTHY LEARY: *Turn on to the internal neurological energy.... Tune in means to harness up the new revelation and energy.... And drop out, now this may sound like reckless advice today, but it's the oldest advice that philosophers and religious leaders have passed on. Detach. Drop out. Find what's within. Turn on, tune in, drop out. And I stand by that statement.*

PEGGY HITCHCOCK: *Traditionally all these substances have been used as sacred substances, and my problem with Tim was a philosophical one when he started proselytizing by saying "Turn on, tune in, drop out." I thought that without any preparation, without any direction, it was a contradiction of everything that we had worked with in the early days of using psychedelics, always under circumstances that were very controlled and being with people who were of like mind and who had experience. And in a setting that was very nurturing. Saying "Turn on, tune in, and drop out" always seemed irresponsible. He was a professor, he had an academic background, and in a way, he threw out the baby with the bathwater.*

In 1968, Leary was again busted for pot, this time by the California State Police during his abortive run for governor against the incumbent, Ronald Reagan. He had the support of people like John Lennon, who wrote the Beatles' tune "Come Together" for the campaign.

Named "the most dangerous man in America" by President Richard Nixon, Leary insisted the marijuana found in his car had been planted.

YOU HAVE TO BE QUITE A BADASS TO GET LOCKED UP FOR YOUR IDEAS.

TIMOTHY LEARY: *One evening I was in a parked car and a policeman came up to the car and opened the door against my wishes and made a pass at the ashtray and said, "You're under arrest for, uh..." I said, "For what?" He said, "For marijuana." And he reached in his pocket and pulled out two joints I'd never seen before, half joints, and said, "You're under arrest."*

He was finally jailed in 1970, one of the first casualties of the War Against Drugs. But when he was given the very same personality assessment he himself had devised at Berkeley in the 1950s, he was able to answer in a way that got him assigned to a minimum security prison.

ZACH LEARY: *You have to be quite a badass to get locked up for your ideas.*

Then . . . he escaped! He pulled himself hand over hand across a twenty-five-foot-long high wire over a twelve-foot-high chain link fence topped with barbed wire. The Weather Underground, a far-left militant revolutionary organization, disguised him and got him and Rosemary out of the country. He was on the lam for a year and a half, first spending time with a group of Black Panthers led by Eldridge Cleaver in Algeria, and then in Switzerland, before being captured in Afghanistan.

REPORTER: *Can you comment on your plans now?*

TIMOTHY LEARY: *My plans are to work for the Black Panther Party for the overthrow of the American government.*

TOP: Leary in Switzerland on the run.
ABOVE: Joanna Harcourt-Smith. Photo by Robert Altman.

* * *

ROSHI JOAN HALIFAX: *When we crossed paths in Algeria he didn't look like he was having that much fun. Eldridge Cleaver looked definitely distressed. And it didn't look like they were enjoying each other. But I think Tim played with every edge.*

JOANNA HARCOURT-SMITH: *Who Timothy Leary was for me in the beginning, he was just a song of the Moody Blues: [singing] "Timothy Leary's dead, no, no, no, no . . ." Little by little I got this romantic image that this Timothy Leary might be,*

> # ISOLATION IS NOT ONLY TO KEEP SOMEBODY IN A BOX BUT IT'S ALSO SO THEY UNLEARN TO COMMUNICATE WITH THE OUTSIDE WORLD.

you know, like the king of outlaws. Through a series of extraordinary coincidences, I met Timothy Leary in Switzerland and found out that he was a fugitive from prison. I was twenty-six years old and I found that very exciting. It felt like it was my destiny to meet him, and I was ready for anything with him. . . .

I was taught that a woman's place was to find the alpha male, the most interesting, powerful, rich male around. But to me, it translated to, okay, find the most interesting man in the world. And at that time, he was one of the most interesting men in the world. . . .

He spoke about his life in terms of being imprisoned and escaping. He said that he was in prison and he escaped and he went to Algeria with his wife Rosemary. Then he went to Switzerland instead of being imprisoned by Eldridge Cleaver and his politics, and once again he was imprisoned by a gangster and his machinations. Rosemary left him while they were in Switzerland, and I think he was very sad about that. I think he absolutely adored her.

We flew to Afghanistan from Vienna, and when we got to the airport in Afghanistan, an attaché of the American embassy stole our passports out of Timothy's hands and this incredible ordeal started.

I was taken with him back to California, where I'd never been. It was a perfect PR coup for Nixon. Two days before the inauguration we got brought back in front of hundreds of journalists, so Nixon had the front page: "Timothy Leary brought into custody."

JOANNA HARCOURT-SMITH: *I began to see this man come out of his solitary confinement cell somewhat confused, very red eyes. He told me that they probably fed him drugs in the food that they were giving him. They let me visit*

ABOVE: Leary being interviewed in Folsom Prison.

him when he was in a padded cell. He was in a straightjacket. His head was shaved. And he began to change in the sense that there was less and less and less of Timothy Leary on the outside. Isolation is not only to keep somebody in a box but it's also so they unlearn to communicate with the outside world.

For those of you who know him, he's relaxed and looks well. But behind the camera sits the warden, the assistant warden, and probably the captain of the guards. I am Joanna Leary, and I'd like to see him out of here as quick as possible.

REPORTER: *What do you think of your future? Do you think you're going to walk out of Folsom Prison a free man one day?*

TIMOTHY LEARY (IN FOLSOM PRISON): *I think my future is very interconnected with the future of this country. You just can't keep your philosophers in prison. If I am kept in prison, it's going to be a very bad symptom for freedom and for hope and for union!*

* * *

ANDREW WEIL: *Criminalizing use and possession of drugs doesn't work and makes everything worse. I don't think we can suddenly legalize things overnight. I believe in education as the key to rational drug policy, and that means being honest about their positive effects as well as negative effects, being honest about the drugs whose use we not only tolerate but promote, like alcohol and tobacco, and that we make money from, our government makes money from, so it's real education, truthful education, and I think it has to be at all levels of society.*

JOANNA HARCOURT-SMITH: *Timothy decided to turn state and federal evidence so he would get out of prison. He was released on April 21, 1976. The next morning the feds came and said, "We've received news that people want to kill you, both of us, and so you have to go into the Witness Protection Program." Timothy insisted that they bring us to Santa Fe. Our names were changed to James and Nora Joyce.*

ABOVE: Leary and Joanna Harcourt-Smith in the Witness
Protection Program in Pecos, NM. Photo by Bill Eppridge.
BOTTOM: Photo of Leary by Baron Wolman.

*We were two drunks lost in the wilderness,
trying to encounter each other. The loneliness,
the separation, the isolation, had driven my
alcoholism and my drug addiction to an
excruciating place. And so we fought a lot.
We both had suffered so much. And from
where I look at it right now, I think that the
right move for him was to blame me.*

*I don't blame people who were afraid of us.
I do not think there can be absolute change
without anarchy.*

In the end, Leary spent almost four years in
jail, two and a half of which were in solitary
confinement. But no matter how dark the circumstances, in relation to the media he
always remembered that Marshall McLuhan had advised him to "Wave reassuringly.
Radiate courage. You must be known for your smile."

TIMOTHY LEARY: *I've been in forty jails on four continents . . .*

RAM DASS: *I haven't even been busted yet.*

RICHARD ALPERT TO RAM DASS

AFTER REALIZING that Millbrook was truly over for him, Alpert went to France and England for a while. Back in the United States, he moved to the wild west of California, where the counterculture scene was heating up with Kesey's Acid Tests, with LSD provided by the underground chemist Owsley Stanley, and the Grateful Dead was the house band (Owsley was the band's engineer).

Alpert lived with Steve and Barbara Durkee and others in a communal scene. The Durkees were now devotees of the Indian spiritual teacher Meher Baba, who was becoming concerned about the drug use of his followers and sent a message that they were not to take LSD. Alpert wrote a letter defending LSD to Meher Baba, who replied that acid experiences were "far removed from

OPPOSITE: Painting of Ram Dass by Alex Grey.

Reality," and told him he could take LSD three more times, then should stop completely. Dick thought, "What does he know? Nice old man in India, never took acid."

Owsley introduced Dick to Caroline Winter, a beautiful Brit who was Charles Darwin's great-granddaughter, at the Fillmore Auditorium at a Grateful Dead concert. Caroline was his longest relationship with a woman, although he still snuck out to pick up young men. They moved to New York in the fall of 1966, and one of their first visitors was David Padwa, who had sold his company (Basic Systems) to Xerox. With time and money, he'd toured northern India. Now, he told Dick, he was planning an overland adventure in Asia via Land Rover.

Richard was flush with cash. He'd become Owsley's main distributor of the infamous White Lightning LSD, but he was starting to get paranoid about drug dealing. And he was disillusioned with the egos in the psychedelic scene. Where was the lasting transformation

TOP: Ken Kesey. **ABOVE:** Richard and David Padwa.

they'd expected from psychedelics? He told David he would go with him. Maybe he'd meet someone in India who could read what he called "the maps of consciousness."

Meanwhile, Richard visited his mother in the hospital. She had been fighting leukemia for years and was very embarrassed by her enlarged spleen, which made her look pregnant. Everyone around her was in denial about her approaching death. Richard was tripping on mescaline. When he was alone with her, his mother said, "You know, I'm going to die. What do you think death is?"

He replied, "It seems to me, the way you and I are connected isn't really defined by this disintegrating body . . . Your body is decaying before us, but the way you and I love each other, I believe that love transcends death." It was the first time they had communicated as souls, as Ram Dass would say, not as their respective roles.

David Padwa had various delays before setting out for India, so Alpert joined Tim in a series of lectures and events. A week after the Human Be-In in Golden Gate Park, his mother died at the age of sixty-four.

A few months later, Caroline and Dick went to the mountains of northern New Mexico, where Steve and Barbara Durkee (along with Jonathan Altman) had purchased land for a commune where all spiritual traditions would be honored, called the Lama Foundation. While staying on the beautiful land, Caroline and Richard realized that although they were in love, his bisexuality meant their physical relationship was not going to work in the long term. And David Padwa was finally ready to go. As the Summer of Love kicked in, Alpert was ready to move on and explore India.

ABOVE: Ram Dass (far right) in Kausani, India.

Richard met up with David and the Land Rover in Tehran, Iran. They drove through the Afghanistan countryside to Kabul, through the Salang Pass, and visited the huge Buddhas carved into the cliffs in the Bamiyan Valley that were later destroyed by the Taliban. Finally reaching India, they partied on houseboats in Srinagar in Kashmir and trekked to Amarnath, a cave sacred to Lord Shiva high in the Himalayas. (Later, Maharajji told Ram Dass, "You went to Amarnath, but you didn't know what it was.") Then they went to Dharamsala, where they had an audience with His Holiness the Dalai Lama and talked with him about LSD and consciousness.

They went on to Benares, where they watched bodies being cremated on the banks of the Ganges River. In a boat on the river, they took LSD and saw the bloated corpse of a young child bumping against the side of the boat (young children were often put in the river when they died instead of being burned). It made a big impression on Alpert about the nature of impermanence.

As they traveled, Richard gave LSD to any holy man who wanted to try it, hoping one of them could offer him understanding. One old Buddhist monk said, "It's good, but not as good as meditation." Another just wanted to know where to score more acid. Alpert was getting depressed by the time they got to Kathmandu in Nepal. The trip was at an end, and they planned to go to Japan next and meet Alan Watts and Gary Snyder in Kyoto.

At the Blue Tibetan restaurant, they met a tall Western *saddhu* (renunciate) with a blond beard, his hair in dreadlocks. Michael Riggs was a twenty-three-year-old surfer dude from Laguna Beach. He'd been in India for years and was now called Bhagavan Das. They took LSD and hung out together for days. Not ready to leave India just yet, Richard was sure this Western yogi knew something, and asked to travel with him. He was also attracted to Bhagavan Das, who in turn was attracted to Alpert's stash of LSD.

They set out together, barefoot. Whenever he tried to tell Bhagavan Das stories about his life, the six-foot-seven-inch yogi would say, "Just be here now." After several

ABOVE: Neem Karoli Baba, also known as Maharajji.
LEFT: Bhagavan Das.

months, Bhagavan Das said he needed to go see his guru about his expired visa and asked if they could retrieve the Land Rover to drive into the Himalayan foothills. That night, Alpert went outside to use the outhouse and stared up at the stars above. Suddenly he felt the presence of his mother.

The next day they drove to a small temple on a steep hillside. He followed Bhagavan Das to where an old man, wrapped in a plaid blanket, sat surrounded by about twenty people. The old man said, "You came in a big car? Will you give it to me?"

Bhagavan Dass immediately said, "Maharajji, it's yours." Richard freaked out. The car was David's! Then the old man said, "You were out under the stars last night. You were thinking about your mother. She died last year. She got very big in the stomach. Spleen, she died of spleen."

Richard's mind went into paranoid overdrive, then simply gave up. He felt a violent wrenching in his heart and started to weep. He realized that if this old man knew about his mother's spleen, then he must know everything about him—his sexual double life, his intellectual pretense . . . but all he could feel coming from Maharajji was pure unconditional love, and all he kept saying to himself as he sobbed was, "I'm home."

ABOVE: Maharajji and Ram Dass. Artwork by Nathan Kubes.

He was moved into a nearby temple, where he would spend the next six months learning from Hari Das Baba spiritual practices like yoga and meditation, and occasionally getting to meet with Neem Karoli Baba, Maharajji.

RAM DASS: *My guru is about a seventy-year-old man. I don't know anything about him, really. You know, I don't even know that he exists, really, but it seemed to me that there was a little old man in a blanket, and when I looked at him, the first time I looked at him I thought, I wasn't going to be hustled, and the second time I looked at him all I wanted to do is touch his feet.*

I looked up, and he was looking at me with unconditional love, and I had never been looked at with unconditional love by anybody. I felt love, I felt love, and I felt something happening in my heart.

Thrilled that he had "finally met someone who *knows*," he was able to give Maharajji a hefty dose of Owsley's White Lightning LSD (three pills, over 900 micrograms), when Maharajji asked for "the yogi medicine." Alpert watched and waited. And nothing happened. Nothing at all. Maharajji's consciousness was way beyond LSD. The strongest tool Alpert had found for accessing higher states of consciousness had no effect at all on Maharajji.

LAMA TSULTRIM ALLIONE: *When we were taking LSD in Golden Gate Park with the Grateful Dead in 1966, early '67, we felt that there was hope that we were*

ABOVE: Ram Dass and Maharajji.

going to change the world in some way. What we were seeing was so powerful, that if anybody would just take this LSD, they would change. And many, many people did. Somehow, I was on the crest of that wave, and I was at the right age to ride that wave in. I was also very fortunate to go to India at the same time that Ram Dass did for the first time in 1967, and to meet teachers. My teachers were Tibetan; his were Hindu. But we all had this, "Oh, here are the people that did this without drugs."

RAM DASS: *He [Leary] trained me in the beginning of my escape, and Maharajji then took over. I see them as my two powerful teachers in escape artistry.*

Maharajji gave Richard a spiritual name, "Ram Dass," which means "servant of God," and gave his *ashirvad* (blessing) for his book. What book, Ram Dass didn't yet know.

RAM DASS: *In India, they call the great saints the living dead. And I find that fascinating that they have died to life and there they are. And that's sort of what I experience, not in the reduced sense of being impoverished by it or what happened to the joy and the preciousness, sweetness, because I feel a lot of passion in my life. But I am also dead. I'm also empty. I'm also empty.*

I BELIEVE THAT LOVE TRANSCENDS DEATH.

TOP: Ram Dass in New Hampshire in the film *Sunseed* by Frederick Amertat Cohn.

ABOVE: Ram Dass at Sculpture Studio. Photo by Michaeleen Maher.

JOHN PERRY BARLOW: *And he comes back and he's maybe eighty pounds lighter and is putting on a lot of holy man airs, which is particularly grating having seen him in his previous manifestation. You know, I'm thinking, same guy, new schtick.*

Over time, Leary was dismissive of Dick Alpert's spiritual journey, which he saw as his merely playing lieutenant to yet another prophetic master.

RALPH METZNER: *Leary did not like gurus, period. Leary thought Alpert's transformation into a guru was absurd, you know, like a joke.*

RAM DASS: *Timothy seemed quite comfortable with the metaphors of the religious traditions. But later those became grist for the mill of his revolution also. And he treated me sort of like an old-fashioned type person. . . . by the time he was busy not respecting me in print or publicly, I was so comfortable in what I was doing that I no longer used Timothy as an arbiter of my validity as a human being, which I had earlier on. I mean, you give people power to tell you where you are. And he and I had used up that role relationship.*

ROSHI JOAN HALIFAX: *Stan Grof and I got married in '72 and then I met Ram Dass, after his transformation from Richard Alpert. Nice Jewish boy, Harvard professor, cellist, intellectual, radical, and by that time he was Ram Dass. And I really loved what he was doing.*

BE HERE NOW

The former Harvard professor was now a yogi. He was invited to speak at Wesleyan University in March 1968. Everyone expected him to talk about psychedelics and psychology, and they were taken aback when Alpert walked in barefoot, with a bushy beard, dressed in his white robe, and carrying his *mala* (prayer beads). He sat down cross-legged and talked about Maharajji, yoga, and consciousness, connecting psychedelics with deeper spirituality.

Later that spring, he gave a series of sixteen talks at the Sculpture Studio in New York. Transcriptions from that event birthed *Be Here Now*, which became a manual for spiritual seekers around the world. It was first published in 1970 as *From Bindu to Ojas* by the Lama Foundation—a limited edition with hand-stitched pages and hand-stamped artwork in the central brown pages of the book. Profits from the book went to the Lama Foundation, turning it from a residential commune into a large retreat center for spiritual renewal and discovery, hosting teachers from the East and interreligious dialogue.

Soon, *From Bindu to Ojas* was reformatted and published as *Be Here Now* by Random House. It has sold over two million copies, and is *still* in the top five books on spiritualism on Amazon.

TIMOTHY LEARY: *You can tell me, where did "Be here now" come from? That was you!*

RAM DASS: *Be here now?*

TIMOTHY LEARY: *Yeah. You've heard of that haven't you?*

RAM DASS: *Yeah.*

TIMOTHY LEARY: *You invented that.*

RAM DASS: *Yeah. Well, but it was actually Bhagavan Das, who every time my mind would go off into my Jewish neuroticism he'd say, "Look, just come back here and be here now." So I took it as a title, but he used to say it to me.*

JUST BE HERE NOW.

LAMA TSULTRIM ALLIONE: Be Here Now *was seminal. It's still seminal, it's still opening up young people's minds. They get that book, and it does what it did to us so long ago; it's amazing. Ram Dass was a bridge between East and West and was a major person to open this gateway of Eastern wisdom to Western culture.*

ANDREW WEIL: *I got a tape of a Ram Dass lecture and heard the whole story of Maharajji and India and how he became Ram Dass. That made a very strong impression on me. Then I got the book. I would say reading* Be Here Now

I WOULD SAY READING *BE HERE NOW* AND HEARING HIS STORY WAS ONE OF THE MAIN THINGS THAT MOTIVATED ME TO START DOING YOGA, TO START MEDITATING, TO REALLY CHANGE MY WAYS.

TOP LEFT: *From Bindu to Ojas*, the original *Be Here Now*, published by Lama Foundation in 1970. **TOP RIGHT:** *Be Here Now* paperback published by Lama Foundation in 1971.

and hearing his story was one of the main things that motivated me to start doing yoga, to start meditating, to really change my ways. He was a great inspiration to me and, since then, he was a teacher to me in an odd way. He was someone who had been out there in ways that were bigger and more intense than I was.

Be Here Now came out while Ram Dass was with Maharajji on his second trip to India. Other Westerners, inspired by Ram Dass in the United States, had also found their way to India and to Maharajji.

LIFE GOES ON

(1970s–1990s)

ONCE LEARY'S long struggle with the FBI and the Justice Department was concluded, and he and Joanna had parted ways, in December 1978 he married his fifth wife, Barbara Chase, and adopted her son Zachary. They settled in Los Angeles, where Leary had some small roles in movies, wrote books, did the lecture circuit . . . and in a Leary-esque twist of fate went on a speaking tour with G. Gordon Liddy, also now an ex-con.

ABOVE: Tim and fifth wife, Barbara Chase, and four-year-old son Zach Leary.

RAM DASS: *Timothy drank a lot, but I don't remember him getting drunk. He was the romantic Irish bard, a kind of itinerant scholar, the kind of rascally person at the bar, the charming guy that in one of his yearbooks had under his picture, "Girls, worry no more." He had this Irish charm that was very, very seductive. Women were a big part of Timothy's life all the way through his life. There was a lot of loss, but I don't think that was the key issue. The key issue had to do with a way in which a connection with a woman brought him into balance.*

ZACH LEARY: *Timothy Leary married my mother when I was four years old. He was the father who raised me from the age of four until he died, when I was twenty-two years old. I lived with him for seventeen years. Somebody pointed out to me once that I have the great distinction of living with him longer than anybody else did . . . ever. He was just a very standard white-picket-fence father with me. Most people don't know that, and when I tell people it's really a surprise. I mean, he took me to Little League practice; he played baseball with me in the yard; we went to Dodgers games all the time; he made sure I did my homework. It was, you know, shockingly normal.*

Ram Dass came back into Tim's life after the Harvard reunion in 1983. All throughout the '80s, Ram Dass was around. I have many great stories of the two of them together, and some very special ones of the three of us together that are huge imprints in my life. They remained close throughout that time and they had a great admiration for each other. In many ways Tim was really Ram Dass's first teacher, and he still holds Tim in high regard. Every time I go to see Ram Dass, all I want to do is talk about Maharajji and all Ram Dass wants to do is talk about Tim . . . happens every time.

TOP: Tim and G. Gordon Liddy after becoming friends in prison.
ABOVE: Young Zach Leary.

Leary and Ram Dass reconnected in 1983 at a reunion at Harvard for the Harvard Psilocybin Project. Neither Ram Dass nor Tim regretted leaving Harvard or the separate paths they had taken after Millbrook, and both were happy to become part of each other's lives again.

RAM DASS: *He didn't ask me for legitimacy of his life, and I didn't ask him for legitimacy of mine. That allowed a new kind of respect to emerge between us, which was interesting. It was a respect that honored our differences rather than the adventure of sharing an idea. And I felt that Timothy really respected me in the end and I certainly respected him.*

TIMOTHY LEARY: *The last twenty years have been remarkable. They have put us through changes.*

RAM DASS: *Yeah.*

TIMOTHY LEARY: *And we have put them through some changes!*

[laughter and applause]

TOP: Robin Williams, Zach, and Tim showing off their catch. **ABOVE:** Ram Dass and Tim at Harvard Reunion.

ZACH LEARY: *When I became a teenager, fourteen or fifteen years old, the floodgates opened and I was taking LSD. My dad was probably the best person around at the time to talk to about LSD. There was no one who could talk about it better or more eloquently than he could, with some real gravitas and*

credibility. Here he was, a very serious Harvard professor who turned on and changed his life. Naturally, and through the lens of the media and pop culture, he became this incredible spokesperson for it because there was no one better to do it, really. No one more qualified to do it. He was also extremely self-aware that he was so charismatic and that he was a performer. He really knew that he had the gift to go out there on stage and convey a message. I don't think he set out to become that guy, but he was the best one at being the guy.

In the '80s, Leary's mind was blown in another way by computers, the internet, and virtual reality. As he said in his book *Chaos & Cyber Culture*, "the PC is the LSD of the 1990s."

RAM DASS: *What is the whole thing you've been talking about—freedom of communication?*

TIMOTHY LEARY: *Everything we were doing was communication, right?*

RAM DASS: *Yeah, well . . .*

TIMOTHY LEARY: *Interpersonal, interpersonal. Everything I've done, remember the little checklist and all that to get people to communicate? The web is my dream come true. There's a kid in North Korea or South Korea and he says, well, we don't have enough money. They go to any school . . . with a telephone you can afford the equipment to allow that classroom to be online.*

RAM DASS: *In other words, ultimately, it is a democratization of information and all of that. It's a great leveler. Does this next generation have enough sense of community or connection to keep stable structures at all, or is that . . . ?*

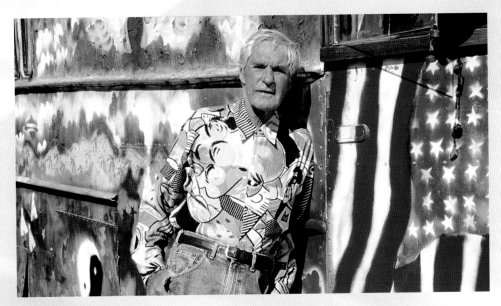

ABOVE: Photo of Tim by Lisa Law.

TIMOTHY LEARY: *Well, what's a stable structure?*

RAM DASS: *I don't know. How anarchic can it get, or . . .*

TIMOTHY LEARY: *Imagine that is not anarchism, but freedom.*

RAM DASS: *It's freedom.*

TIMOTHY LEARY: *Yeah. Anarchy is . . .*

RAM DASS: *And freedom is the line between chaos and cosmos, or something sort of right at that edge?*

TIMOTHY LEARY: *[laughter]*

LAMA TSULTRIM ALLIONE: *Timothy came into the picture for me as a person rather than as this myth of psychedelics after I had disrobed as a nun and gotten married. Naropa University had been founded in 1974 by Chögyam Trungpa. Ram Dass taught there when it opened. I went to Boulder in 1978, when Leary was there teaching. He was radical, but seemed very caught up in himself, sort of fascinated by himself, and had no spiritual path. He had gotten stuck in the drug as an answer rather than drug as an opener. He wasn't developing, whereas Ram Dass was really on a path. That was a way they were different, yet they shared a history that blew open my generation. They blew open this world, this psychedelic world for us.*

By 1993, Timothy and Barbara had divorced, although Tim remained close to Zach, whom he had adopted.

> MAHARAJJI'S BASIC TEACHINGS HAD BEEN TO LOVE EVERYONE, SERVE EVERYONE, REMEMBER GOD, AND TELL THE TRUTH.

ZACH LEARY: *He had a lot of personal heartache in this life. His wife Marianne killed herself and every marriage ended in divorce. His daughter Susan also committed suicide. Jack didn't speak to him. So there was a lot of heavy stuff going on, a lot of heavy karmas and a lot of interpersonal relationships that he just really couldn't work out. I think that it really broke his heart. There's no question that him getting to raise me was a chance for him to do it over again.*

He had an uncanny knack of reinventing himself. He was much more of a cyberculture icon than he was a '60s hippie icon. That's why he kept young people around, because he was so fascinated with youth culture and with computer culture and early internet culture and cyberpunk culture and music culture and art.

HUSTON SMITH: *Tim liked wine and he liked women and he liked publicity. A kind of a complicated human being. The basic storyline is clear. What he was at heart was an Irish rebel, and he got kicked out of everything he went into. He was kicked out of West Point. He was kicked out of Harvard. He was kicked out of Zihuatanejo. He was kicked out of the United States. And he went to Switzerland and was kicked out of that. He and Ram Dass were friends, but then they parted. Fundamentally different paths of life. Tim was a hedonist and Ram Dass was into service for others.*

ABOVE: Ram Dass at Seva meeting. Larry and Girija Brilliant to left of Ram Dass.

Ram Dass had been busy traveling to give talks and retreats, including fundraisers for the Seva Foundation, a global nonprofit eye care organization he cofounded in 1978. He had searched different pathways and reexamined his commitment to service. Maharajji's basic teachings had been to love everyone, serve everyone, remember God, and tell the truth.

As he wrote in *Being Ram Dass*: "Service as a spiritual path lacks glamour. I liked moving in and out of planes of reality, esoteric teachings, secret mantras, meditations in caves, experiences of bliss.

TOP: Ram Dass and Stephen Levine leading meditation at a retreat. **ABOVE**: Ram Dass with Stephen and Ondrea Levine.

Those experiences of different planes originated in my use of psychedelics, and I'd grown attached to those experiences. It was another subtle trap that I created for myself, another kind of spiritual ego."

And so, determined to face the nitty-gritty of life, he headed straight for the greatest fear in the West—death and dying. He had been a kind of midwife to the dying since 1963, offering wisdom, compassion, and his knowledge of other planes of consciousness.

Ram Dass, together with Dale Borglum (who had also been with Maharajji in India and today runs the Living/Dying Project) and Stephen Levine (author of *Who Dies?* and *A Year to Live*), thought America was ready for a place where people could come to die consciously. With money from Ram Dass, Dale started the Dying Center in Santa Fe, New Mexico, in 1981, and was the one who ran it.

ABOVE: Tim with teenage son Jack.

> # MY PAINS I TREAT LOVINGLY. PAIN—A WORTHY ADVERSARY. WE'RE GOING TO HAVE TO FIGHT IT OUT.

ROSHI JOAN HALIFAX: *Ram Dass was the pioneer. He's the person who really opened up that field for me personally. The work with dying people is something that we do here at the [Upaya] Zen Center. It is really critical to train healthcare professionals in compassionate care. But what Ram Dass did was inspire people to bring spirituality and existential questions into their awareness so that they could not only die well, but also live well.*

RAM DASS: *The cost in keeping people alive—forget quality of life now, just physically alive—the intensive-care-unit strategy was getting prohibitive and eating up all the resources. Then came the hospice movement, which said what we missed was that the psychological part of dying is also important, and*

hospice is much cheaper than the intensive care unit. All it requires is that we accept the fact that death exists. And that's a big shift to accept death existing versus it's a failure and an enemy.

The AIDS epidemic started in the early '80s. Because of his own sexuality, Ram Dass felt called upon to help. In *Being Ram Dass*, he said: ". . . working selflessly with no thought of gain, I was still a bit removed until I got down in the trenches with AIDS. It was the first time I experienced death on that scale. Seeing the terrible progression of HIV as it tore apart people's lives ripped open my heart, too. I found myself committed on a more emotional level than before to help in whatever way I could." During these years Leary went through some very personal pain. His daughter, Susan, had committed

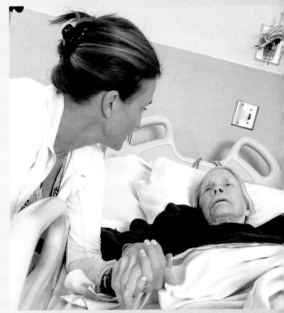

ABOVE: Gay Dillingham with her mother, Ruth, in hospice.

suicide, like her mother had, after a long struggle with mental health issues. Jack, his son, was estranged from what had been his mostly absent father. Tim stayed close with his son Zach, but Barbara had divorced him. And then came the news of his late-stage, inoperable prostate cancer.

TOP: Ram Dass in ocean in Maui.
ABOVE: Dassima and Ram Dass.

Not long after Leary's death, in February 1997, Ram Dass suffered a severe stroke and a massive cerebral hemorrhage. Doctors gave him only a 10 percent chance of survival. Hundreds of hours of rehabilitation later he was still partially paralyzed, though able to get around in a wheelchair. He called it "fierce grace." Six months after the stroke, Mickey Lemle filmed the documentary *Ram Dass, Fierce Grace*, showing Ram Dass's spirit coming through his rehabilitation trials. After years of service to others, he now had to learn to accept help. Although physically restricted and often in pain, he continued his work, furthering the vision of expanded consciousness he had pioneered with Timothy Leary more than forty years earlier.

RAM DASS: *I'm more now identified with my soul, and more compassionate to my body, because the stroke was hard on it. The stroke was so painful that I pushed it out of the way by going to the witness in the soul . . . just witnessing the stroke rather than experiencing the stroke. My pains I treat lovingly. Pain—a worthy adversary. We're going to have to fight it out.*

ROSHI JOAN HALIFAX: *He has been through a lot. It's interesting to be with him, because there's an absence of self-pity there. And the way he handles his pain and the fact that he's been in that chair for fifteen years, I mean, that is no joke, and he's over eighty now. It's really remarkable that he's lived so long. It's a testimony to his delightful determination that I think is a model for all of us.*

The lush tropical island of Maui became Ram Dass's healing environment. Swimming in his pool and on Mondays at a gentle beach, he enjoyed the freedom of his body in water.

Surrounded by friends, caretakers, and under the ministrations of his assistant, Dassima, he carried on with his work, including twice-yearly retreats for 400 participants at a time that mixed Buddhist mindfulness teachings with Hindu devotional practices.

After decades of helping to raise Timothy's children, Ram Dass discovered in 2009, at the age of 78, that he, too, was a father. He received a letter from someone saying his older brother looked exactly like Ram Dass, and that his mother, Karen Saum, had once mentioned this brother might have a different father. Karen had been a graduate student at Stanford when Dick Alpert was teaching there, and they'd had a brief affair for a few weeks. Karen had moved back east and never told Richard about her pregnancy. DNA tests confirmed that Peter Reichard, born in 1957, was Ram Dass's son. Peter was married, with a teenage daughter, so Ram Dass was a grandfather as well.

As he said in *Being Ram Dass,* "I was astonished by the news. I had explored spiritual love for decades, but the direct emotional connection between parent and child was outside my experience. . . . I thought of myself as a spiritual uncle, a loving elder. Now here I was, a blood father to a fully adult human being. This was an unforeseen turn on the path. Wow."

TOP: Ram Dass and Oprah in Maui. **CENTER**: Ram Dass at Age Nation conference. **BOTTOM**: Ram Dass with his son, Peter Reichard.

ROSHI JOAN HALIFAX: *Wow! In a million years, of all the crazy things. And what a great guy, Peter, his son.*

Ram Dass said, "This enigma of DNA and karma, the biology of the West and the inner sense of the East, fascinates me. How these waves of incarnations, and the winds of grace, shift our lives! I love that I am a father. It has given me the opportunity to cultivate part of my being I didn't think would be touched in this life . . . I see how love for a child can become soul love."

SOUL

THE SLIVER OF OPPORTUNITY

RAM DASS: *Do you use the word soul?*

TIMOTHY LEARY: *Soul?*

RAM DASS: *Yeah. You've used it a lot.*

TIMOTHY LEARY: *All the time!*

RAM DASS: *What do you mean by it?*

TIMOTHY LEARY: *It's the conscious . . .*

RAM DASS: *. . . the consciousness?*

TIMOTHY LEARY: *Superconsciousness, and it/she hangs around the brain.*

RAM DASS: *In cryonics, what do they do? Do they open the skull and take the brain? Is that what they do? Or you're having the whole head cut off? What do you do?*

TIMOTHY LEARY: *To tell you the truth, I'm not that clear because that technology is very rudimentary. It's growing now. They have frozen dogs. It's dog time. A way of uncertainty. That's what you want on your watch, right? It means, who gives a fuck what time it is, right? [Ram Dass was wearing a watch that had the tau character (τ) for every hour.]*

RAM DASS: *Tau time. Yes.*

TIMOTHY LEARY: *You don't care what time it is?*

RAM DASS: *No, it's to remind me not to care what time it is.*

TIMOTHY LEARY: *I love that.*

RAM DASS: *Every time I look at it.*

TIMOTHY LEARY: *My kind of guy.*

RAM DASS: *In this whole cryonics business, what is the probability that you will, as a brain, experience some kind of solution?*

TIMOTHY LEARY: *Brought back?*

RAM DASS: *Oh, well, not necessarily brought back here, but be conscious of the air?*

TIMOTHY LEARY: *I don't think so.*

RAM DASS: *No?*

TIMOTHY LEARY: *It's that fifteen minutes I'm interested in. I'm trying to popularize the notion that when your heart stops and you have your brain going for two to fifteen minutes—and maybe we can extend it—I'm going to be taking oxygen. I want to find out what are the foods that the brain needs. Because the body exists to pump up stuff that the brain needs, right?*

RAM DASS: *I see.*

TIMOTHY LEARY: *That is the territory. The sliver of . . .*

RAM DASS: *This has nothing to do with cryonics? This is before cryonics.*

TIMOTHY LEARY: *I want to talk about this period of settling in.*

RAM DASS: *Okay. Yeah, go ahead, tell me, tell me.*

TIMOTHY LEARY: *They call it the sliver of opportunity—that period when your heart stops and you're free from your body. And all of the reports, we said it before, that going down for the third time, your life flashes in front of you and you . . .*

RAM DASS: *Total ecstasy.*

TIMOTHY LEARY: *. . . saw the light at the end of the tunnel. Yeah, that all comes from near-death experiences, so space is not practical.*

RAM DASS: *Right, okay. Let's just say awareness in space without body.*

TIMOTHY LEARY: *Yeah.*

RAM DASS: *Could it be without brain?*

TIMOTHY LEARY: *I call the brain my soul.*

RAM DASS: *Yeah, but I'm saying after you freeze a brain, let's say . . .*

THEY CALL IT THE SLIVER OF OPPORTUNITY—THAT PERIOD WHEN YOUR HEART STOPS AND YOU'RE FREE FROM YOUR BODY.

TOP: Graphic by Colin Gill. **ABOVE:** Graphic in *From Bindu to Ojas.*

TIMOTHY LEARY: *Well, I'm freezing my soul.*

RAM DASS: *You're freezing your soul?*

TIMOTHY LEARY: *And will my soul come back, is that it?*

RAM DASS: *Let's say you didn't freeze your brain, it just got eaten by worms, okay? Is there any awareness independent of that? Is there any subtler form of energy?*

TIMOTHY LEARY: *I don't know.*

RAM DASS: *It's possible though, isn't it?*

TIMOTHY LEARY: *Yeah. I'm very conservative, see. I'm interested in things that are here and now.*

RAM DASS: *I know you are. Isn't it interesting how you and I are that different?*

TIMOTHY LEARY: *I'm very practical.*

RAM DASS: *Why did it end up that you're interested in things here and now and I'm interested in la-la land all the time? Why is that?*

TIMOTHY LEARY: *You're not really . . .*

RAM DASS: *I am, I am. Well, what happens after the brain gets eaten?*

TIMOTHY LEARY: *If you know what happens in those fifteen minutes when your body goes . . . That's the time your brain can really tell what's left of it, see. At least I am ignorant about something important.*

RAM DASS: *Are you going to do something to send messages back?*

TIMOTHY LEARY: *Well, we won't discuss that in public. [laughter]*

RAM DASS: *You see some value in sending back a message about what happens in those fifteen minutes.*

TIMOTHY LEARY: *Yes, I think it's valuable to the species. But we learn more about reactions.*

RAM DASS: *I understand.*

TIMOTHY LEARY: *I think the human race and the brain want to be freed to do more, and the body is a vehicle for the brain.*

RAM DASS: *I agree. I would think the brain is a vehicle for the awareness.*

TIMOTHY LEARY: *Yeah. I agree. That's my cop-out too. If there is such a thing as a soul, or whatever you want to call her; she hangs around. Not the sole of your foot. She's gonna hang around the brain.*

RAM DASS: *Well, Ramana Maharshi says it's right here in your heart.*

TIMOTHY LEARY: *The heart. I had to tell a thousand Hindu girls that the heart is a wonderful organ to pump blood; they haven't discovered Harvey's theory of circulation. They're using the heart for metaphor.*

RAM DASS: *Yes. They're using the heart as a metaphor.*

TIMOTHY LEARY: *It's a very bad metaphor, I think.*

RAM DASS: *They're using the lower right-hand corner, the size of a thumb, the . . .*

TIMOTHY LEARY: *Are you kidding me?*

RAM DASS: *No.*

TIMOTHY LEARY: *Wow.*

ABOVE: Zach and Tim.

RAM DASS: *It's the size of a thumb, it's called the* hridayam, *the heart cave, and it's right here.*

TIMOTHY LEARY: *It grows there? Naturally?*

RAM DASS: *It's right there, it's there, it's there. But it's not in a physical manifestation.*

TIMOTHY LEARY: *Oh, I see.*

RAM DASS: *It's in a subtle form.*

TIMOTHY LEARY: *Well, how do you contact it?*

RAM DASS: *Well, you gotta get better technology.*

TIMOTHY LEARY: *Yeah, yeah. Better than LSD?*

RAM DASS: *In LSD you saw all that, but it went by so fast that you didn't have a model, a conceptual model to save it. It just went through.*

TIMOTHY LEARY: *So much went through every time I took acid—must be for you too—that what we've conceptualized is the tiniest trivia of the edge of the whole thing, and that's why dying seems so fascinating to me.*

RAM DASS: *Exactly.*

TIMOTHY LEARY: *Because you're going like, whoosh. It may not be like that, but I hope it is.*

She hangs around the brain. She doesn't hang around the kneecap or underneath your socks.

RAM DASS: *No, no. Okay. She hangs around the brain.*

TIMOTHY LEARY: *Yeah.*

RAM DASS: *And how does she use the brain, or does the brain use her?*

TIMOTHY LEARY: *Well, I can't pretend—*

RAM DASS: *Do they just make love, or what do they do?*

TIMOTHY LEARY: *I think they're probably the same thing. But I get in trouble with the spiritual people.*

RAM DASS: *That makes sense. Yes, I understand. [laughter] I mean, what are you saying, that the eternal soul is a brain?*

TIMOTHY LEARY: *I say, well, how about your God? Does your God have 120 billion neurons and each neuron is connected to 10,000 others? How many connections does your God have? Probably not even on the internet. [laughter]*

RAM DASS: *My God is the internet, my dear.*

TIMOTHY LEARY: *I know, my darling. I know.*

Ram Dass wrote about the soul in *Walking Each Other Home* (with Mirabai Bush): "The individual soul is the *jivatman,* and the big soul, the supreme soul, is *atman. Jivatman* is finite and conditioned, while *atman* is infinite and eternal, the indestructible divine existence. . . . I am identified with my soul, yet I am still a separate entity. The next step is for me to dive into the ocean, to become one with the All. At the end of life, my soul will fully merge with the atman and become one with it. . . . Death, you see, is the full transformation from identification with the ego ('Doctor, doctor, save me') to becoming one with the soul."

Timothy thought about the soul this way (in *Chaos & Cyber Culture*): "The closest you are probably ever going to get to navigating your soul is when you are piloting your mind through your brain or its external simulation on cybernetic screens. Think of the screen as the cloud chamber on which you can track the vapor trail of your platonic, immaterial movements. If your digital footprints and spiritual fingerprints look less than soulful on the screen, well, just change them. Learning how to operate a soul figures to take time."

THINK FOR YOURSELVES. DISCOVER, EXPLORE, AND TREASURE YOUR OWN UNIQUENESS; THE PROPER STUDY OF HUMAN BEING IS YOURSELF.

ZACH LEARY: *He was a lifelong intellectual, a lifelong scientist, and I don't think he would go on record talking about what he thinks the soul is or if the soul has a life after its incarnation in our body. I don't really think he would. He liked to dismiss those things because his access to enlightenment was through the mind, was through intellectual realization. That was his yoga. But again, I think he was much more spiritual than we ever knew.*

TIMOTHY LEARY: *Think for yourselves. Discover, explore, and treasure your own uniqueness; the proper study of human being is yourself.*

RAM DASS: *Tim's right. Go into yourself, and then if you go in deep enough there is truth and that truth leads you to pick the people, the beings, with whom you're going to spend your life and your death.*

TIMOTHY LEARY: *We've covered a lot of stuff. Are you satisfied?*

RAM DASS: *And we have laughed a lot, haven't we?*

TIMOTHY LEARY: *We have. We've had a great time.*

RAM DASS: *And there's no way we could fake a love of this sort.*

TIMOTHY LEARY: *Can you have dinner with us afterwards?*

RAM DASS: *I can't. I've gotta fly back to San Francisco.*

TIMOTHY LEARY: *Oh. Darn.*

RAM DASS: *I'm working against a deadline for a book. A deadline. You're working against a deadline too.*

TIMOTHY LEARY: *A hell of a deadline. Yeah. Yeah.*

RAM DASS: *Speaking of deadlines . . .*

TIMOTHY LEARY: *Richard, you have enriched my life. I'm sorry; Ram Dass, you have enriched my life.*

RAM DASS: *No, I can be Richard. Come on, I've been Richard to you.*

TIMOTHY LEARY: *You've enriched my life, Richard, and I'm so proud of both of us. I thank you for making this opportunity for us to make love in public.*

RAM DASS: *Yes. Exactly. Thirty-five years we've been dancing like this. It's been a hell of a dance, hasn't it?*

TIMOTHY LEARY: *And we're totally different, not totally different. Yeah, it's been great.*

RAM DASS: *But at this moment we so appreciate each other, isn't that nice?*

TIMOTHY LEARY: *Big hug . . . [kisses] Okay,* **CUT.**

DEATH

ΛΠD ΙΠ ΤΗΣ ΣΠD

TIMOTHY LEARY: *Dying is a taboo topic. It's shocking. People don't expect you to talk about their dying or to plan it. Certainly the greatest adventure, the celebration of your life, should be the process of moving on. Living's a team sport, dying's a team sport. When I knew I was dying, and I knew I was going to die actively and creatively, I called Ram Dass because I knew he would understand, and*

ABOVE: Photo of Tim by Lisa Law.

he has been my amused guide, counselor. It's like calling Dad or your older brother, although I'm much older than he is.

RAM DASS: *In 1963, Tim and I, with Ralph Metzner, were working on* The Psychedelic Experience, *a manual based on* The Tibetan Book of the Dead, *and that led to a pretty deep study, along with psychedelics. And since we were both dealing with what we considered psychological death and rebirth, and we had been through those death/rebirth experiences many times together, it was reasonable for him to think of me as somebody who would understand what this death experience was going to be like for him. The fact is, I've been working with death and dying since 1963 as a very major part of both my spiritual practice and my service. I think that also would lead Timothy to feel that I would understand the process he was going through.*

But as Tim Leary said, "I die so hard each time." He was talking about the psychological death. He was also talking about his physical death. You're used to feeling safe and secure as a separate entity. Every time there is the dissolution of beliefs, of structures, of conceptual reality, there is going to be incredible fear.

ABOVE: *Ram Dass Overlooking Los Alamos* by Dean Chamberlain.

ROSHI JOAN HALIFAX: *The question "Am I afraid to die?" is something I actually live with every day.*

PEGGY HITCHCOCK: *I think everybody's afraid to die. The question is how do you deal with the fear.*

ZACH LEARY: *I like being alive. I like this incarnation. You know, I'm attached to it.*

ANDREW WEIL: *If I weren't afraid to die I would not be taking it seriously. I mean, in some ways I think death is the most important experience that you're preparing for all your life.*

RAM DASS: *I've seen so many people die clinging to the past and also worried about the future. I think, this is the moment. That's what I get is this moment. And one of these moments, I'll be dead. And that'll be the moment.*

I often equate dying with a maha acid trip, you know, huge. When I take a very strong dose of LSD, at first I'm waiting and waiting and waiting; then it starts to happen. My consciousness starts to liquefy; I start to play with alternate planes of consciousness. Then it's going faster and faster, and then you don't have a place to hang on to anymore with your identity. It's the dying process of the psychological realm, dissolving the perspective you see from where you're standing. And that is one of the things that's happening while people are dying. We haven't created the right space for people not to be afraid during this moment that can be very frightening, because we're so identified with our separatenesses that we don't see that getting into a universal consciousness is an incredible, wonderful journey.

ANDREW WEIL: *In the dying process there's often a lot of fear. And I think psychedelics make it possible to step aside from that and observe what's happening dispassionately. A guided psychedelic experience in a dying person often enabled that person to drastically cut doses of opiates for pain relief, which kept consciousness clear. It often greatly facilitated communication with family and friends where before there was no honest communication about what was going on. And it made the dying process easier. These were strongly positive results of these studies.*

LAMA TSULTRIM ALLIONE: *The feeling about LSD was okay; it was an experience that was mind-opening, but it didn't stay, and there needed to be that groundwork, that deeper spiritual discipline to not only reach those states that we had reached before, but also to go beyond that to stabilize it . . . and to put ourselves in the position at the time of death where we could make a conscious transition.*

RAM DASS: *It's inconceivable to me that Timothy could have taken as much acid as he's taken and been through as much as he's been through and end up a philosophical materialist, in which when the body is dead, you're dead. Yet that's what he professed. In the last telephone conversation I had with Timothy, he said, "Richard, I think I'm losing my mind." I thought that was interesting. He said, "I think I'm losing my memory. You know, memory is almost everything," which is exactly what a philosophical materialist would say. Then he said, "No, there's something more than memories," which, of course, is the whole realm I live in. He was silent for a moment, then he said, "But I forgot."*

I loved it! That was such perfect Timothy, to play with my consciousness and to play with his own that way.

TIMOTHY LEARY: *I'm going to write a book about senility and growing old and the memory thing. Just as a child, you learn how to make the connections of Mama and two and two is four.*

RAM DASS: *As you get old, you let them go.*

TIMOTHY LEARY: *Oh, yeah. It goes.*

RAM DASS: *It goes. But what doesn't go? See, the consciousness doesn't go, but the associative mind goes.*

TIMOTHY LEARY: *Everybody gets the death that they deserve.*

YOU'RE USED TO FEELING SAFE AND SECURE AS A SEPARATE ENTITY. EVERY TIME THERE IS THE DISSOLUTION OF BELIEFS, OF STRUCTURES, OF CONCEPTUAL REALITY, THERE IS GOING TO BE INCREDIBLE FEAR.

RAM DASS: *No doubt.*

TIMOTHY LEARY: *And everybody gets the life they deserve.*

RAM DASS: *Me, as a karmacist . . .*

TIMOTHY LEARY: *But I'm tuning psychologically into this life, not the next life. Because all that karma shit is like the Christians say, if you do this down here, you'll get rewarded up there. But we're talking about instant karma.*

RAM DASS: *Right now. Yes.*

TIMOTHY LEARY: *Be here now karma. [laughter]*

RAM DASS: *Yes, yes. [laughter] So we can interpret "Be here now" the way we want to.*

TIMOTHY LEARY: *You're supposed to.*

RAM DASS: *Yeah. So tell me about senility.*

TIMOTHY LEARY: *That as my mind loosens, life becomes an adventure.*

RAM DASS: *Doesn't it? Yeah, yeah. Because you're not carrying so much time-binding material.*

TIMOTHY LEARY: *I try to popularize so people can explain it. In my lecture to an old people's home, I said, "Senility is like the effects of very good marijuana." Short-term memory loss, see, like you're driving around stoned, but you forget where you're going?*

RAM DASS: *Many times.*

TIMOTHY LEARY: *But you don't care.*

RAM DASS: *You don't care because you're already there. Well, that's what I've been telling people that work with people with Alzheimer's. Because it seems to me that if you relax and don't demand linearity, everybody gets happy.*

TIMOTHY LEARY: *Enjoy it.*

RAM DASS: *Everybody gets happy. And if you demand, "Oh, Maude, come on back. You remember . . . ," everybody gets nervous and uptight.*

TIMOTHY LEARY: *Yeah. Short-term memory loss. Long-term memory gain. And then the basic thing is you don't give a fuck.*

CANCER

TIMOTHY LEARY: *I found out I had cancer about a year ago, but the real pressure of it, the symptomatic pressure of it, just the last two or three months. I've had moments of deep pain. I've had moments when the pain pills almost knocked me out and I was a source of worry to my friends because I was suffering so much. I had never experienced much pain and it has been a shock to me to discover that pain exists and can really dominate your consciousness, so I've had to work that through.*

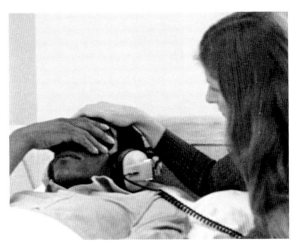

ABOVE: Joan Halifax with patient dying of cancer.

RAM DASS: *See, the issue is pain and consciousness. The relation of pain to consciousness, when you're looking at it from just the physical body, the goal is to get rid of as much pain as possible even if you have to put the person to sleep and keep them asleep till they die. That's the most humane thing to do. To me, the secret of pain is to come into the moment, because it takes you out of time. Time seems to minus me, to be the corrosive element in the picture.*

TIMOTHY LEARY: *Yep. But see, time is a body thing. It's light and dark and sleep and wake and moving your bowels.*

RAM DASS: *So, is my sense of the continuity of awareness beyond the brain just my wanting to keep something going?*

TIMOTHY LEARY: *I don't have that.*

RAM DASS: *I know you don't have it. You're curious. I'm curious, too.*

TIMOTHY LEARY: *I'm very curious.*

RAM DASS: *But it'd be interesting. At some point we're gonna meet and one of us is going to say . . .*

TIMOTHY LEARY: *There's no way we can lose, right?*

RAM DASS: *No.*

TIMOTHY LEARY: *Actually, this is a win-win proposition.*

RAM DASS: *We shouldn't have prostate cancer at all.*

TIMOTHY LEARY: *My orgasm level started going down around fifty.*

RAM DASS: *I see. Okay, I'm gonna get to work on it again.*

TIMOTHY LEARY: *Keep your orgasm rate up. Use it or you lose it, meaning use your prostate or you lose your life. I am also trying to understand cancer. This whole thing; some friends who've ended up with cancer say I'm gonna beat it, I'm gonna fight it.*

RAM DASS: *Oh, no. Make love to it.*

TIMOTHY LEARY: *Damn right. You and I understand it. Very few people . . . They think I'm crazy to say I want to know more about it. She's the mystery lady.*

RAM DASS: *Sure, sure. It's a vital, alive thing in your body.*

TIMOTHY LEARY: *You are one of the few people that I can share that with. That's an interesting level we play at. Cancer is a mystery. I've become very friendly with my cancer. Also, I see cancer now as my teacher, and I try to talk to her and make friends. I don't want to get her angry. I say, Miss Cancer, we're in it together. We're both stuck in the same body. Let's make a deal. Let's keep the body alive a little while and we can have some more fun.*

RAM DASS: *That's as good a healing technique as I've ever heard, actually.*

TIMOTHY LEARY: *Well, I learned it from you.*

RAM DASS: *It's a very good healing technique.*

TIMOTHY LEARY: *It's common sense.*

RAM DASS: *Yeah, of course.*

TIMOTHY LEARY: *Cancer's like my neighbor. I'm a Bosnian and she's a Serb, or something like that. But the whole attitude of fight, fight, fight . . .*

RAM DASS: *I know. Instead of embracing, you work out a deal and live compatibly together.*

> # CANCER IS A MYSTERY. I'VE BECOME VERY FRIENDLY WITH MY CANCER. ALSO, I SEE CANCER NOW AS MY TEACHER, AND I TRY TO TALK TO HER AND MAKE FRIENDS.

TIMOTHY LEARY: *And, of course, I'm not saying that my cancer talks to me like UFOs, but it's an attitude. 'Cause I love my cancer. I'm not worried about it. And it's worry and anxiety that kill.*

RAM DASS: *Yes, yes.*

TIMOTHY LEARY: *One thing. I've really been anxious. And I'm not an anxious person.*

RAM DASS: *No, I don't feel that at all.*

TIMOTHY LEARY: *You were, but you're not anymore. You used to be more anxious.*

RAM DASS: *I don't know how I'll be if I'm in your situation. At this moment, I don't feel anxious at all, I mean about my life or anything. When it comes to things like pain or fatigue or stuff like that, I can still go under into it and get pained or fatigued or angry or something. You know?*

TIMOTHY LEARY: *Me, too. Old men get cranky.*

Doctors Roshi Joan Halifax and Stan Grof were among the first to research the use of psychedelics with the dying, in their case terminal cancer patients, in 1967.

ROSHI JOAN HALIFAX: *Stan and I worked on the LSD project with people dying of cancer [at Spring Grove Hospital in Maryland]. That was really powerful. Everything in my own life really came into a fluid, open moment, very fluid open moment around three streams: psychedelics, Buddhist practice, and engaged practice or being socially engaged. What Ram Dass did for our culture was to open up a door of spirituality that was so radical and so beautiful and characterized by such extraordinary love that he made all doorways available to people. Whether you were a Buddhist or a Jew or a Muslim or a Hindu, whatever dharma door you were going through, Ram Dass, in one way or another, blessed that door by having surrendered so completely to love.*

CRYONICS

TIMOTHY LEARY, at seventy-five, approached his final days with characteristic enthusiasm. He promised to "give death a better name or die trying." Some years earlier, Tim had investigated cryonics —removing and freezing his brain at the time of his death—so it could be preserved and transplanted into a healthy body if that became possible.

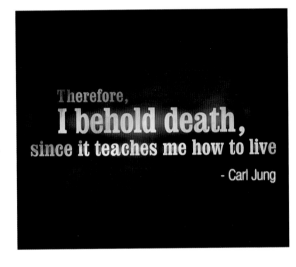

Therefore, **I behold death,** since it teaches me how to live
- Carl Jung

RAM DASS: *In cryonics, what do they do? Do they open the skull and take the brain? Is that what you're gonna do?*

TIMOTHY LEARY: *To tell you the truth, I'm not that clear, because that technology is . . .*

RAM DASS: *Very rudimentary, isn't it?*

TIMOTHY LEARY: *Yeah. It's growing now. I know this is corny, it's pathetic, but the first ships were rowboats. Every technique that science has now for bringing you back I've signed up with. I'm going to have my blood cells available for cloning.*

Timothy expounded upon his ideas about the brain in his book *Chaos & Cyber Culture* (1994): "The human brain is, by auto-definition, the most powerful control communication unit in the known universe. A constellation of a hundred billion cells floating in an ocean of info-gel. The brain has no muscles and no sense organs. It is a shimmering sea swarming with microchip molecules packaged in enormous hardware neurons, all linked by chemical-electrical signals. We could not understand how the brain operates until our electrical engineers had built computers. And now we are learning how to beam our brain waves into the Cyberia of electronic reality, to think and play and work and communicate and create at this basic (0/1) level."

ABOVE: *Tim Leary at Home* by Dean Chamberlain.

HE PROMISED TO "GIVE DEATH A BETTER NAME OR DIE TRYING."

TIMOTHY LEARY: *At this period in human history, we're lucky enough to be here, when, for the first time, scientists are developing ways to keep you alive or to bring you back. The church would say, "No, you have no right. Your body belongs to God!" Well, show me the paperwork.*

ZACH LEARY: *Cryonics seemed like a great idea on paper, and why not? I mean, go for it. And like he always used to say about it, it's the second stupidest thing you can do in the world; the first is letting your body get eaten by worms. When it came down to the end, we didn't like the invasion of privacy that was going on at the house with the cryonicists. It felt a little like weird science, God-complex kind of stuff. And we weren't really prepared, I guess, to have that sort of invasion of privacy.*

RAM DASS: *I think he got attached to being in control in life and therefore didn't plan the end as well as he might have. He wanted to be in control and then drink the potion as Socrates had done and then say goodbye and then die. In fact, he didn't do that and I like that ending because I think what it showed was that death is more than anything anybody plans, which I love.*

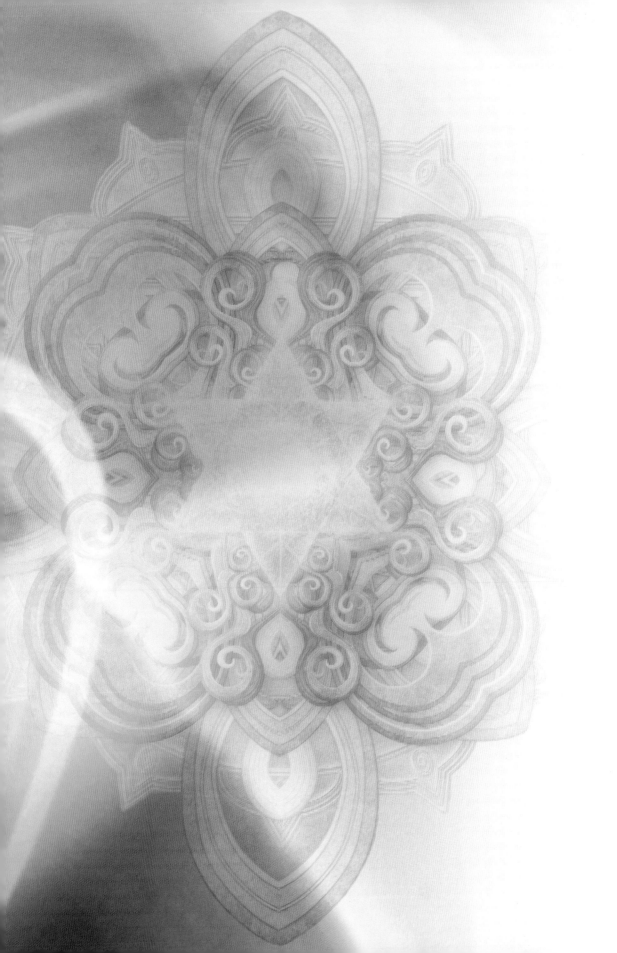

THE DYING PROCESS

RAM DASS: *The moment of death is the moment when you engage the deepest mystery of the universe, and that's what the whole of Eastern traditions is about—preparing you for that moment so that you will be equanimous, you will be curious, you will be present, you'll be nonclinging to the past, not grabbing but just being with each moment. Moment by moment. Some people do their most profound spiritual work in the last few minutes before they die.*

ABOVE: Photo of Tim by Lisa Law.

I do a kind of a continuous spiritual practice that is one in which I keep expanding into awareness, and the definition of Ram Dass and a body and of all of that just become phenomena that are appearing and disappearing. I practice continually going in and out of this. Part of that is in anticipation of the moment of death, when I assume this will happen the same way. I'm eighty years old, I . . . no! My body is eighty years old; I am a soul. There's no doubt at all that I will be around after I die.

RAM DASS: *What happens at the moment of death when the mind separates from the body? Are we any closer to describing that process of thinking? Where do you go?*

TIMOTHY LEARY: *To every mistake I make, like when they put me in the freezer and the electricity goes out, see? That means you have to have double fuses. I don't care about coming about, but I'd like to leave a track record that my grandchildren and great-grandchildren could live a better life with less fear. And you do the same thing. When you said, "Be here now," you were popularizing* *this ancient, ancient thing. And that's the genius gift that both of us have. We can popularize these concepts and make them appealing.*

RAM DASS: *I think you're doing a great deal to cut through the fear of death. But to die at that moment, fully conscious, to me that's been the history and the yearning of all Eastern religious traditions. To, at the moment of death, aaah, there goes . . . Like when Allen said, "I don't feel anything in my legs, now I don't feel anything." Remember that? Under acid?*

TIMOTHY LEARY: *Sliver of opportunity, or, there's a sliver of the process of dying.*

RAM DASS: *The sliver of opportunity to slide through in consciousness.*

TIMOTHY LEARY: *Your body has gone. And all this talk the Buddhists have about getting out of the body. . .*

RAM DASS: *. . . It has gone. You've dropped your body. Now the question is, who dropped the body?*

TIMOTHY LEARY: *Well, that's another question. I'm talking about the time when your heart is gone. Your body is gone.*

RAM DASS: *Okay, okay.*

TIMOTHY LEARY: *The brain is up there. Twenty years ago, we knew almost nothing about the brain. Now we know 120 billion neurons. Every neuron in your brain has ten thousand connections. It's going to take us decades to begin to understand the magnificence and complexity of this brain, which creates the realities we inhabit. My brain says we're happy when we get rid of that body, then we don't have to worry about shitting and the career and all that. The brain is happy 'cause then the brain is in the state that the Buddhists talk about. It's pure consciousness.*

RAM DASS: *Sure. It's extricated itself from all the senses.*

TIMOTHY LEARY: *And it's going to come to a point, 'cause when your brain stops, that fifteen minutes is timeless because you can't measure by how . . .*

RAM DASS: *Yes, I understand that.*

TIMOTHY LEARY: *Like an LSD session. You go through ninety-five lifetimes and death.*

RAM DASS: *Oh, every minute is timeless.*

TIMOTHY LEARY: *There you go, yeah.*

SOME PEOPLE DO THEIR MOST PROFOUND SPIRITUAL WORK IN THE LAST FEW MINUTES BEFORE THEY DIE.

TOP: Photo by Alan Kozlowski.

ABOVE: Photo of monk by Alan Kozlowski. LEFT: Bicycle Day animation by Centro Sperimentale di Cinematografia.

TIMOTHY LEARY: *Long before I knew I was dying, we were using this metaphor of leaving your body, leaving your mind, and contacting a different level of altered states, expanded consciousness, which now we feel is located in the brain. My life has prepared me for this. I wrote this book on dying twenty-five years ago, and much of the stuff I'm saying now I was writing about when I was in prison in the '70s. It's nothing new for me. I am approaching my stages of dying with incredible fascination and interest and anticipation because, well, I'm going to die. We're all gonna die. Why not learn how to do it with class and style and friendship, as a climactic expression of a life?*

LAMA TSULTRIM ALLIONE: *At the time of death, there's a process that takes place. This period that Timothy Leary speaks about—this fifteen- to twenty-minute period—is what still would be called the process of dying in the Tibetan teaching. So you're not dead yet. The gross body is dead, but the subtle body is still remaining in the body, so that's not yet the bardo. There's a flash of the experience of totality, and that's called the chonyi bardo or the "bardo of suchness," a vast luminous expanse of intelligence, of cognition. If you can realize that, that's when you can be liberated. If you miss that moment—and most people miss it because* *it's just a flash and because of the attachment and grasping—usually the mind then grasps and you move on to the next part of the bardo.*

There's a kind of blackout period for about three days, and then as you come to, you're in what's probably best described as a dream-like state. When you hear people talking about the bardo in the Tibetan sense, that's what they're usually referring to. There are various peaceful energies appearing, and wrathful energies appearing, and so on.

There'll be a kind of being drawn toward that energy field and then toward your parents. Some people say we choose our parents, but from a Buddhist point, it's not quite like that. It's more like we are propelled through karma toward these certain energies in the same way that we don't choose our lives. They say in the Tibetan teachings that a fragile human life is difficult to achieve and easy to lose, this precious human life.

THEY SAY IN THE TIBETAN TEACHINGS THAT A FRAGILE HUMAN LIFE IS DIFFICULT TO ACHIEVE AND EASY TO LOSE, THIS PRECIOUS HUMAN LIFE.

RAM DASS: *From what I understand about the way in which planes of consciousness are shed, whether you look at it as in the Tibetan system or in the Hasidic, the Kabbalistic system, or in many mystical traditions, there is a dissolution of one plane after another. And in each case, when you get too frightened by that dissolution or too fascinated by it or attached to it, it tends to solidify. It's what karma is. It tends to project forward that slight turning of the consciousness.*

GRIEF

RAM DASS: *I do a lot of grief work with people, and what I often find myself saying to people who have lost their child or their spouse after many years is you will grieve and grieve and grieve and you will come up for air and you'll think it's all over and you'll be strong and then you'll go back under and you go through depressions. Let it all run its course. Your mind will recite all the ways you've lost the person, that you'll never have the smell of their body or all these things . . . milk it all. Don't push it away.*

But there will come a time when your mind will quiet down a little bit. And in the quietness of that moment, all the love that you've ever tasted with that person will be living and present and then you'll realize that what the essence was that made you connect with this person has nothing to do with death. That love transcends death, basically. You're going to have to find it out for yourself, but it's true.

JOHN PERRY BARLOW: *I had this tragic loss, the great love of my life dropped dead on me. I was getting this huge overflowing of love from other people and it was just useless. I mean, I felt like a black hole for love, It didn't make any difference what anybody said . . . they didn't understand what it felt like and it felt like they were wasting their love on me. Which is a terrible feeling. I mentioned this to Ram Dass. I said I feel like a bottomless well where love goes and you never hear anything hit bottom. He said, well, consider that it's not bottomless, but it's just very deep, and that one day it will fill with love. I dunno, that still kinda gets me.*

LAMA TSULTRIM ALLIONE: *Death and someone dying is an initiation that we as human beings go through. It enriches us; it deepens us; it opens our hearts. It's a terrible thing but it makes us bigger and deeper and more compassionate as people.*

RAM DASS: *My guru once ate a big meal late at night, and then he went to sleep. Around two in the morning, he woke everybody up at the temple and said, "I've got to have dal and chapati [lentils and flatbread]." The fires had gone out and they were trying to explain to him that he didn't really need it, that he ate a big meal. He was screaming, "I've got to have it. I've got to have it." They built the fires and they made the dal and they made the chapati, and he ate like he'd never eaten before. Then they all went back to bed. They'd say, "Well, who can understand the ways of the guru?"*

The next day, they were sitting at darshan with Maharajji when somebody came in and said, "We've rushed here to tell you that so-and-so died last night."

Maharajji turned to the mothers and said, "You see? That's why I needed the chapatis and dal." They didn't know what he was talking about. Like he was talking to children, he said, "As he was dying, he wanted chapatis and dal, and I didn't want him to have to take another breath just for that." He took on the karma off the . . . I don't know. See, that's an interpretation. All we really have is the phenomenon of his saying all that. I don't know why he said it, but it's a great story.

* * *

When I first went to India, I thought, "It's a great place to visit, but I'd hate to grow old and die there." I couldn't wait to get back to the United States, where I felt safe. Over time, I began to see that in India, death was so much part of life. People died at home. They were carried through the streets on the way to the burning ghat. They saw the fires burn the bodies. It was all out. Old people were there. Everybody was around. Nobody was sent to Florida for their own good.

I realized that the United States is a great culture to visit, but I'd hate to grow old here. It has a very dysfunctional mythology. As we brought death out of the closet, now we can bring aging out of the closet too. Because in this culture, it's not all right to age. It's a failure. Well, we're in a nontraditional society, which is a tricky thing because, in a nontraditional society, everything's changing so fast. I mean, I can't tell you how to hook up the latest software because I'm too old, really. Elder wisdom is not valued in a knowledge culture. It's only valued in traditional cultures, where there is a lineage of passing down wisdom. We don't value wisdom. We value knowledge, and knowledge becomes extinct very quickly.

> I REALIZED THAT THE UNITED STATES IS A GREAT CULTURE TO VISIT, BUT I'D HATE TO GROW OLD HERE.

LEARY'S DEATH

TOWARD THE end of May 1996, Leary began to show signs of kidney and liver failure. Timothy Leary's last trip began early on May 31, 1996. He was surrounded by friends. In the end, Timothy had chosen to die a natural death. He was not cryonically preserved, having cancelled his contract on May 6, three weeks before his death.

ABOVE: Celebration at Leary's home two months before he died.

ZACH LEARY: *I think Tim was a much more spiritual guy than anybody knows and that he would ever care to admit, because to this day I haven't seen anybody handle death so gracefully. I mean, sure, he didn't like the pain and the sickness and the loss of his physical self. He was a very good-looking man, very charismatic, and I don't think he liked becoming so decrepit and sick.*

I think some of his fears of letting go, of not knowing what was next, sure, I think that scared him. I think he was absolutely normal and understandably human in those moments. But the process of dying, actually slipping into that unknown, was incredibly beautiful for him. He wasn't trying to hang on. He was really going with the organic nature of things. It was everybody else around that was freaking out. The house really kind of got out of control. We probably had too many people around, and a lot of us didn't really know what we were going to do once he died. Ram Dass was really mostly there for us. And he was there for us constantly. It was the counseling he was giving to us that was so precious and meaningful. Ram Dass helped to ground us all and kind of quiet us to the point of just falling in love with the final moments.

ABOVE: Vicky Marshall and Michael Horowitz with Tim.

RAM DASS: *I was talking to them about not trying to engage him, not trying to pull him back, but to let him be wherever he is. They could talk among themselves in the room about all the beautiful things he'd done in life, which is like an old Tibetan practice. And I talked to them about working on themselves to not demand linearity, so that if he comes up with things from different places to let their minds soar so they could be with him as his mind floated through planes of consciousness. I told them to love death as much as they love life, to allow the mystery of the universe to be something awesome and beautiful. I think what we really need to do is reduce our phobias sufficiently to sacralize death, to make death a sacred ritual.*

ZACH LEARY: *I remember so well . . . it was a nice day in Los Angeles and he went out to the back patio and had a couple sips of coffee, glanced at the paper, and five minutes later wheeled himself back into bed willingly, and that was it.*

The hospice care worker told us, "This is it. He's slipping away now." There was no question in anybody's mind that that day was going to be the last. It was like a beautiful, orchestrated dance, because he ended up dying a little bit after midnight. From about noon on, we held vigil. People came to say their goodbyes.

I TOLD THEM TO LOVE
DEATH AS MUCH AS
THEY LOVE LIFE, TO
ALLOW THE MYSTERY
OF THE UNIVERSE TO BE
SOMETHING AWESOME
AND BEAUTIFUL.

There was just the process of him detaching from his body slowly, slowly, slowly, saying his last words and taking his last breaths. The whole why/why not, why/why not thing happened several hours before he died. It was sort of, "Should I stay or should I go? Should I stay? Should I go? Why? Why not? Why? Why not?" That's how I took it in at the time. It really felt like he was playfully wrestling with merging into the infinite. Especially during the last couple of weeks, he would call them sneak peeks, where he would kind of lose consciousness for a second and slip into a little mahasamadhi state, where he got a little sneak peek into what death was going to be like. And "why/why not" was him dancing with that.

DEAN CHAMBERLAIN: *Sometime in the last seven hours of his life he said, "Compadre," and then he said, "Esparando" ("I'm waiting"). Then he said, "Follow, follow," and then he said, "Beautiful, beautiful," and then he said, "Flash, flash." Then he said the word why in a deeply moving way—"Why, why?" followed by an almost mantra-like repetition of the words, "Why not?" At least sixty times he said, "Why not?"*

RAM DASS: *It feels like such a statement of release to me, Why not? Why not? Why not?*

* * *

The night that Tim died, I spoke to the family, and then early in the morning I flew to Kalamazoo, Michigan, for a conference on death and dying. By the end of the day, I had dozens of messages on my answering machine from CBS and CNN and ABC, and the Los Angeles Times, and the New York Times, and so on. I thought, I don't want to play this one out, at all. Then I thought, well, I'll try one. I called the Washington Post and was asked, "How do you feel about your friend Timothy's death?" I looked inside to see how I felt, and I said, "Fine." There was this long silence on the other end of the phone. It was clear that they had written the material already and I wasn't playing by the script.

What I meant, of course, was that Timothy and I exist on a plane of consciousness in which dying and dropping of the body was more like which video did you rent for tonight? Obviously I'll miss the Irish wit and charm, his wonderful mind, and the sweetness of his love, but that isn't the real place he and I lived together. We didn't see each other that often, anyway. He's in me—that's where he is. He and I met in ideas and experiences and intuitive being together that is so deep that I can't imagine I will ever think of Timothy as not being present. Timothy and I are explorers, we're beloveds, we're deeply connected to each other and I can't imagine that that'll change a flicker. A flicker.

DAN RATHER [CBS Evening News]: *Here in Southern California, the Harvard professor who became the outlaw acid king of the 1960s is dead. Dr. Timothy Leary advocated the use of mind-bending drugs.*

JOHN PERRY BARLOW [AT LEARY'S WAKE]: *Timothy Leary's dead. Long live Timothy Leary.*

RAM DASS: *The incredible beauty of this moment and of Timothy's life was there like a rainbow. I was so overwhelmed with the beauty of it that I started to sob, and of course everybody immediately thought I was grief stricken.*

Did I learn anything from Tim's death? Well, I did. First of all, I learned something about these metaphors of dying, because coming into Timothy's home, it was coming into a world that was so homogeneous, really, in the way it was looking at death, which was a different metaphor than the one that I would usually be involved in. The information downloading, the cryonics, the materialist dream, nightmare, whatever you would call it, was so solid and real there that there wasn't much space on one level. There wasn't much space for my metaphors.

At first, I felt shut out by that, and then that only lasted a moment. And then I felt, "Wow, I mean, he's just . . ." What I was seeing were the limits of my own metaphor. He was showing me I just had another metaphor. That was all I had. And it was great because since I surround myself with people who share my metaphor, it begins to seem real, about souls and reincarnation and stuff like that; karma. I teach that all the time. But what level of reality do you teach it from? And then he showed me also about the kind of celebratory nature. He showed me that the culture was lacking in its ability to optimize the quality of life during dying, which meant not only pain reduction but pleasure. It meant not only reflection and contemplation but play and delight and joy. I think Timothy's dying is one of the great dyings. I really do. And I think I'll mark it the Leary way. [laughter] It sounds good. Copyright "Leary way of dying." I learned a lot from that, yes.

I think the way he handled his death very much reflected the way he lived his life, because he turned it into a theater piece; he turned it into a poem; he turned it into a dance. It's what he did with all the rest of his life. I often think, in a funny way, that Mahatma Gandhi's "My life is my message" is a really interesting statement about Timothy. Timothy's basic message was the way he lived his life. And, in effect, what he said on this issue of his dying was, to me, a major cultural statement. He said that it was a celebratory moment, which is not part of our cultural mythology.

Timothy Leary made history one more time, fulfilling his dreams as a futurist. Seven grams of Tim's ashes were sent into space on a Pegasus rocket, along with those of Gene Roddenberry, the creator of *Star Trek*; a Princeton physicist; a cofounder of the International Space University; and others. It was the world's first funeral in space. And Timothy was finally free to soar through the heavens.

RAM DASS (IN *BEING RAM DASS*): *Tim Leary and I didn't just share psilocybin and LSD, we shared an amazing cultural moment of transformation, a collective internal journey that played out on a national stage. The real change that came from psychedelics was not hippie drug culture but opening people to their inner nature, to their soul. Psychedelics were a gateway drug all right, but not to more drugs. They were an opening to the living spirit beyond the materialist and existential constructs of the 1950s. Because of that opening, Eastern philosophy and inner exploration have penetrated deeply into our culture. Karma is now part of the English language, meditation is an accepted practice, and there are yoga studios on every street corner. Kids learn to cultivate awareness as part of social-emotional learning in school, and spiritual practice is a widespread lifetime pursuit.*

TIMOTHY LEARY: *People ask me what's the major discovery about myself and my life. This is a hard question, and I hope discovery is ahead. [laughter] It's the confidence to think for myself and to explore. And I always do it with the guidance and counsel of my friends. Ask the standard questions. Why are we*

here? Where are we going? How can we use this time to best explore and utilize the tremendous gift of our brain?

People ask me if I have any messages or what do I want on my tombstone or my bumper sticker. Well, basically it's think for yourself. Discover, explore, and treasure your own uniqueness. Keep moving and changing with the help of your friends.

RAM DASS: *I'm getting near the end of my life, and I've been getting my heart ready for death. I can't say definitively what happens after death. I just say what I feel will happen. Faith is the whole game. Faith, faith, faith. It was like when I had my stroke, the stroke hit me in my faith and I got depressed. People thought I was depressed because of my body, but I was depressed because my faith was not good. My pains I treat lovingly. I'm loving of them, and I get a relationship of that pain in my soul. There are some pains that are a worthy adversary. We're going to have to fight it out. I think, one, incarnation is wonderful, and, boy, I can't imagine a better incarnation.*

Ram Dass left his body in December 2019 at his home in Maui.

HEREAFTER

THE FIELD OF LOVE

PEGGY HITCHCOCK: *I think Richard's contribution to humanity is one thing and Tim's is another. It's an ongoing impact and I can only hope that it continues; the perceptions that people can have from the psychedelic experience really can be very helpful in realizing our common humanity, and the importance of our interrelationship with everything else in the world—*

every living being, every plant and every tree. It's a very visceral experience and to experience it on a cellular level can be very profound in terms of realizing what we have, and what we can do.

LAMA TSULTRIM ALLIONE: *I would like to say thank you to Ram Dass and to Timothy for their ability and their willingness to go to those frontiers that opened up so much for so many people. I'd like to say thank you to Timothy Leary and to Ram Dass for being so brave and opening the door to these realms that changed the world in so many ways and for their compassionate offering of that to others, to the best of their ability.*

ANDREW WEIL: *Leary and Alpert will be remembered as cultural icons of the '60s and very influential people, not only in American culture but in world culture as well. Ram Dass has been a very influential spiritual teacher, an inspiration to many people. The early work that they did with psychedelics was very important. They showed that set and setting influenced the experience greatly, that the mindset of the experimenters greatly influenced the outcomes, and they demonstrated the positive potential of the use of psychedelics, which just now is becoming a focus of attention again. There are mainstream articles talking about the psychological and physical benefits of psychedelics. It's the first time I've seen this kind of positive press in a very long time.*

ABOVE: Roshi Joan Halifax and Ram Dass.

ROSHI JOAN HALIFAX: *Ram Dass was a pioneer for me in opening up my own sense of the deep value of the spiritual and the existential dimensions in how people die. It's really important because he's elderly and so am I. The horizon of our life is decreasing. Tim is gone; so many of the people that were in the weave of our life. And that the value of relationship is such in my life now as an older person, and I know he feels the same, that it's really important for us to stay connected.*

I felt that he saw that very clearly with Tim. His effort at reconciliation or normalizing—if you can ever normalize a relationship with Tim, or Ram Dass could ever be normal—but how he approached Tim at the end of Tim's life and how they also did their act together prior to Tim's diagnosis in terms of becoming a kind of spiritual-intellectual-trickster-vaudeville act. They were role models of what it is to be a pair of opposites and to play in the field of love.

I look at Ram Dass and Tim Leary in a way like Han Shan and Shide of the Tang dynasty—two trickster-monk-poets who left civil society and became kind of oddballs—iconic figures who stepped off the map and really paid for it. Tim was brilliant, and completely eccentric, and he also just played. I think he was just playing Congress, just playing our government. He was an incredible trickster, a fabulous imposter. Tim played with every edge. He was so radical, he was willing to say anything, do anything, be anything. I was wary of Tim. He was incredibly charismatic and attractive. I wasn't wary of Ram Dass, because he seemed much more undefended and much safer to me. Tim seemed like a wonderfully dangerous person. But there was always this heart connection between me and Ram Dass.

RAM DASS: *I would call Timothy a deeply spiritual man, yes. Oh, absolutely. But what he then did was he put down all that stuff, including me. Timothy's put-down seemed immature from my point of view. It seemed like he didn't have the discipline to go into the metaphor deeply enough to appreciate how subtle it really was. He had bought it at one level and sort of chewed it up and then rejected it.*

Timothy never really meditated. He was a reflector. He was a contemplative, but he was not a meditator. He didn't value extricating awareness from thought the way I do. He loved thought. He loved the play of the mind. He absolutely loved

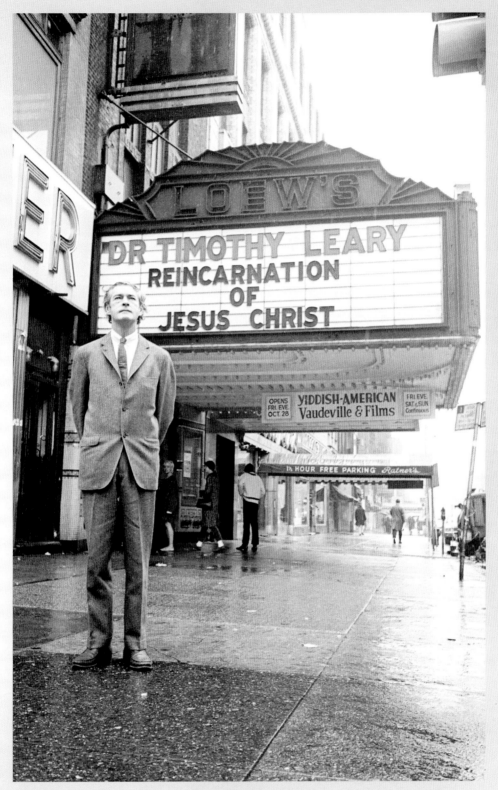

ABOVE: Photo courtesy Everett Collection / Bridgeman Images.

THEY WERE ROLE
MODELS OF WHAT
IT IS TO BE A
PAIR OF OPPOSITES
AND TO PLAY IN
THE FIELD OF LOVE.

ONE BECOMES THE MOMENT. ONE BECOMES LOVE.

it. He adored it. He loved knowing he knew. He loved the delight of intellectual. Aldous Huxley was just the same way. I remember the same quality in him. And I remember Alan Watts once saying to me when we were kind of drunk, "Dick, your problem is you're too attached to emptiness." And I said to him, "You're too attached to form, Alan."

Tim loved words and images and ideas, and I see them as birds flying in the air of silence. It's like figure-ground reversal, whether you're focused on the emptiness or the form. Ultimately form is no other than emptiness; emptiness is no other than form. But that's a very evolved experiential space to be in. I feel that Timothy didn't deny the silence or the emptiness. He just was fascinated by the form. That's really it, his fascination with the form.

If you identify with your soul when you're alive, death is just another moment.

God is awareness. So when we tune in to our awareness, we close the space between the individual and God.

You delve deep into the moment. You come to all and everything.

One becomes the moment. One becomes love.

Life and death are one.

It's ecstatic.

It's like becoming God. Aaah . . .

CONTINUE THE EXPLORATION

IN THE FILM AND IN THIS BOOK, various issues are brought up by Timothy Leary, Ram Dass, and others that we are all "dying to know" more about, especially the taboo against death and dying. How do we change the general cultural perspective that keeps us from a celebratory death—passing from this life with dignity and passing through the bardos with more awareness? Leary and Ram Dass come at this question from their individual philosophical and spiritual points of view from both Eastern and Western thought.

What about the psychological death experienced with psychedelics? The long-lasting War Against Drugs is slowly being dismantled and new scientific research is affirming the benefits of the mind-and-heart opening created by magic mushrooms and other psychedelics, which are once again being studied. Leary's story reflects the misguided government policy that created social disorder, undermined legitimate scientific research, ruined the lives of many who were incarcerated, cost a fortune, increased drug use (of all types), and provided a boon to criminal enterprise.

The governmental and institutional repression of thinkers and scientists like Leary and Ram Dass is typical of a society that fears change. These psychologists-turned-rebels thought for themselves, questioned authority, and paid dearly for those liberties. By extension, society paid dearly for the shortsighted actions of an establishment that sought to preserve power and the status quo. But the hard-earned wisdom of both men remains in the prolific writings, audio, and film offerings each did, as well as those by the others who appear in this book.

To see the film, visit **dyingtoknowmovie.com**

To hear Ram Dass sharing his wisdom, go to
ramdass.org and **beherenownetwork.com.**

TIMOTHY LEARY

Books

- *Interpersonal Diagnosis of Personality* (Resource Publications, 1957)
- *The Psychedelic Experience: A Manual Based on the Tibetan Book of the Dead* (with Ralph Metzner and Richard Alpert) (University Books, 1964)
- *Psychedelic Prayers: And Other Meditations* (Poets Press, 1966)
- *Start Your Own Religion* (Kriya Press, 1967)
- *The Politics of Ecstasy* (G. P. Putnam's Sons, 1968)
- *High Priest* (World Publishing, 1968)
- *Jail Notes* (Douglas, 1970)
- *Neurologic* (self-published, 1973; Leopold Classic Library, 2017)
- *Confessions of a Hope Fiend* (Bantam, 1973)
- *Starseed* (Level Press, 1973; Leopold Classic Library, 2017)
- *What Does WoMan Want?* (88 Books, 1976)
- *Exo-Psychology: A Manual on the Use of the Human Nervous System According to the Instructions of the Manufacturers* (Starseed/Peace Press, 1977)
- *Neuropolitics* (with Robert Anton Wilson and George A. Koopman) (Starseed/Peace Press, 1977)
- *The Game of Life* (Peace Press, 1979)
- *The Intelligence Agents* (Peace Press, 1979)
- *Changing My Mind, Among Others* (Prentice Hall, 1982)
- *Flashbacks: An Autobiography* (J. P. Tarcher, 1983)
- *Chaos & Cyber Culture* (with Michael Horowitz and Vicki Marshall) (Ronin Publishing, 1994)
- *Turn On, Tune In, Drop Out* (Ronin Publishing, 1999)
- *Change Your Brain* (Ronin Publishing, 2000)
- *Your Brain Is God* (Ronin Publishing, 2001)

Audio and Video

- *The Psychedelic Experience: A Manual Based on the Tibetan Book of the Dead* (with Ralph Metzner and Richard Alpert) (Broadside Records, 1966; reissued on CD by Locust Music, 2003)
- *L.S.D.* (Pixie Records, 1966)
- *Turn On, Tune In, Drop Out: The Original Motion Picture Soundtrack* (Mercury Records, 1967)
- *You Can Be Anyone This Time Around* (Douglas, 1970)
- *Seven Up* (with Ash Ra Tempel) (Cosmic Couriers, 1972)

- *Flashbacks* (Dove Books on Tape, 1989)
- *The Inner Frontier* (with Robert Anton Wilson) (Association for Consciousness Exploration, 1989)
- *From Psychedelics to Cybernetics* (with System 01) (Interfisch Records, 1990)
- *Origins of Dance* (with the Grid) (Evolution Records, 1990)
- *Uncommon Quotes: Timothy Leary* (Pub Group West, 1990)
- *How to Operate Your Brain* (Association for Consciousness Exploration, 1994)
- *Right to Fly* (with Simon Stokes) (PsychoRelic Records, 1996)
- *Beyond Life with Timothy Leary* (Mouth Almighty Records, 1997)
- *Timothy Leary Live at Starwood* (Association for Consciousness Exploration, 2001)
- *Timothy Leary: A Cheerleader for Change* (Association for Consciousness Exploration, 2001)

Software

- *Mind Mirror* (Electronic Arts, 1986)

Multimedia Performances

- During late 1966 and early 1967, Leary toured college campuses presenting "The Death of the Mind," which tried to artistically replicate the LSD experience.
- In the early 1990s, Leary created several films in a form of hypnosis tape he referred to as "Retinal Logic." These included *Think for Yourself, How to Operate Your Brain,* and *How to Operate Your Brain Show*—early examples of binaural entrainment.

Films

- Leary appeared in over a dozen movies and television shows in various roles, as well as more than thirty appearances as himself, including *Dying to Know: Ram Dass & Timothy Leary* (2014)—documentary dual portrait by Gay Dillingham.

RAM DASS
Books

- *Identification and Child Rearing* (with Robert R. Sears and Lucy Rau) (Stanford University Press, 1965)
- *The Psychedelic Experience: A Manual Based on the Tibetan Book of the Dead* (with Timothy Leary and Ralph Metzner (University Books, 1964)
- *LSD: A Journey into the Asked, the Answered, and the Unknown* (with Sidney Cohen and Lawrence Schiller) (New American Library, 1966; WS Press, 2023)

- *Be Here Now* (Lama Foundation,1971; Harmony, 1978)
- *Doing Your Own Being* (N. Spearman, 1973)
- *The Only Dance There Is* (Anchor Press, 1974)
- *Grist for the Mill* (with Stephen Levine) (Orenda Unity Press, 1977)
- *Journey of Awakening: A Meditator's Guidebook* (Bantam, 1978, 1990)
- *Miracle of Love: Stories about Neem Karoli Baba* (E. P. Dutton, 1979)
- *How Can I Help? Stories and Reflections on Service* (with Paul Gorman) (Alfred A. Knopf, 1985)
- *Compassion in Action: Setting Out on the Path of Service* (with Mirabai Bush) (Bell Tower Books/ Crown Publishing, 1991; Harmony, 1995)
- *Still Here: Embracing Aging, Changing and Dying* (Riverhead Books, 2000)
- *Paths to God: Living the Bhagavad Gita* (Harmony, 2004)
- *Be Love Now* (with Rameshwar Das) (HarperCollins, 2010)
- *Polishing the Mirror: How to Live from Your Spiritual Heart* (with Rameshwar Das) (Sounds True, 2013)
- *Walking Each Other Home: Conversations on Loving and Dying* (with Mirabai Bush) (Sounds True, 2018)
- *Being Ram Dass* (with Rameshwar Das) (Sounds True, 2021)

Audio

- *The Psychedelic Experience: A Manual Based on the Tibetan Book of the Dead* (with Timothy Leary and Ralph Metzner) (Broadside Records, 1966; reissued on CD by Locust Music, 2003)
- *Here We All Are* (Yogananda Records, 1969)
- *Love Serve Remember* (ZBS Foundation, 1973; released in MP3 format, 2008)— six-LP set of teachings, data, and spiritual songs
- *The Evolution of Consciousness* (Noumedia, 1973)—three-LP set recorded live in New York City, March 1969
- *Cosmix* (with Kriece) (Waveform Records, 2008)—video-enhanced CD of Ram Dass messages mixed with work by Australian DJ and performer Kriece
- *Ram Dass* (with East Forest) (Aquilo Records, 2019)—featuring the final recorded teachings of Ram Dass

Films

- *A Change of Heart* (1994), directed by Eric Taylor and hosted by Ram Dass
- *Ecstatic States* (Wiseone Edutainment Pty, 1996)
- *Ram Dass, Fierce Grace* (2001), directed by Micky Lemle

- *Ram Dass—Love Serve Remember* (2010)—short film included in the *Be Here Now* enhanced edition eBook, directed by V. Owen Bush
- *Dying to Know: Ram Dass & Timothy Leary* (2014)—documentary dual portrait by Gay Dillingham
- *Ram Dass, Going Home* (2017)—documentary portrait of Ram Dass in his later years, directed by Derek Peck
- *Ram Dass, Becoming Nobody* (2019)—documentary portrait of Richard Alpert becoming Ram Dass and Ram Dass becoming nobody, directed by Jamie Catto

RALPH METZNER

Books

- *The Psychedelic Experience: A Manual Based on the Tibetan Book of the Dead* (with Timothy Leary and Richard Alpert) (Citadel Press, 1964, 1992)
- *The Ecstatic Adventure* (Macmillan, 1968)
- *Maps of Consciousness* (Macmillan, 1971)
- *Know Your Type: Maps of Identity* (Anchor Press, 1979)
- *Opening to Inner Light: The Transformation of Human Nature and Consciousness* (J. P. Tarcher, 1986)
- *The Well of Remembrance: Rediscovering the Earth Wisdom Myths of Northern Europe* (Shambhala, 1994)
- *The Unfolding Self: Varieties of Transformative Experience* (Origin Press, 1998)
- *Green Psychology: Transforming Our Relationship to the Earth* (Park Street Press, 1999)
- *Sacred Mushroom of Visions: Teonanacatl* (editor) (Park Street Press, 2005)
- *Sacred Vine of Spirits: Ayahuasca* (editor) (Park Street Press, 2005)
- *The Expansion of Consciousness* (Regent Press, 2008)
- *The Roots of War and Domination* (Regent Press, 2008)
- *Alchemical Divination: Accessing Your Spiritual Intelligence for Healing and Guidance* (Regent Press, 2009)
- *MindSpace and TimeStream: Understanding and Navigating Your States of Consciousness* (Regent Press, 2009)
- *Birth of a Psychedelic Culture: Conversations about Leary, the Harvard Experiments, Millbrook and the Sixties* (with Ram Dass and Gary Bravo) (Synergetic Press, 2010)
- *The Toad and the Jaguar: A Field Report of Underground Research on a Visionary Medicine* (Regent Press, 2013)
- *Allies for Awakening: Guidelines for Productive and Safe Experiences with Entheogens* (Regent Press, 2015)

- *Ecology of Consciousness: The Alchemy of Personal, Collective, and Planetary Transformation* (New Harbinger Publications, 2017)
- *Overtones and Undercurrents: Spirituality, Reincarnation, and Ancestor Influence in Entheogenic Psychotherapy* (Park Street Press, 2017)
- *Searching for the Philosophers' Stone: Encounters with Mystics, Scientists, and Healers* (Park Street Press, 2018)
- *Alchemical Musings* (Regent Press, 2020)

Audio

- *The Psychedelic Experience: A Manual Based on the Tibetan Book of the Dead* (with Timothy Leary and Richard Alpert) (Broadside Records, 1966; reissued on CD by Locust Music, 2003)
- *Bardo Blues and Other Songs of Liberation* (CD Baby, 2005)

ROSHI JOAN HALIFAX

Books

- *Trance in Native American Churches* (1968)
- *The Human Encounter with Death* (with Stanislav Grof) (E. P. Dutton, 1977)
- *Shaman: The Wounded Healer* (Thames and Hudson, 1982)
- *Shamanic Voices: A Survey of Visionary Narratives* (E. P. Dutton, 1979; Penguin Books, 1991)
- *The Fruitful Darkness: A Journey Through Buddhist Practice and Tribal Wisdom* (Harper San Francisco, 1993)
- *A Buddhist Life in America: Simplicity in the Complex* (Paulist Press, 1998)
- *Being with Dying: Cultivating Compassion and Fearlessness in the Presence of Death* (Shambhala, 2008)
- *Lone Mallard* (CreateSpace, 2012)
- *Standing at the Edge: Finding Freedom Where Fear and Courage Meet* (Flatiron Books, 2018)
- *Sophie Learns to Be Brave* (with Kiersten Eagan) (Bala Kids, 2022)
- *In a Moment, in a Breath: 55 Meditations to Cultivate a Courageous Heart* (Shambhala, 2023)

Audio

- *Thorns and Roses: Living Mindfully* (New Dimensions Foundation, 1987)
- *Being with Dying: Cultivating Compassion and Fearlessness in the Presence of Death* (Audible Studios, 2014)

- *Being with Dying: Contemplative Practices and Teachings* (Sounds True, 2015)
- *The Fruitful Darkness: A Journey Through Buddhist Practice and Tribal Wisdom* (Audible Studios, 2015)
- *Optional Ways of Dying* (with Stanislav Grof) (Big Sur Recordings)
- *Standing at the Edge: Finding Freedom Where Fear and Courage Meet* (Macmillan Audio, 2018)
- *Cultivating the Courage to Love* (with Ram Dass and Frank Ostaseski) (Better Listen, 2021)
- *Stages of the Journey* (with Ram Dass and Frank Ostaseski) (Better Listen, 2021)
- *Cultivating the Courage to Love* (with Ram Dass and Duncan Trussel) (Better Listen, 2021)

Video

- *Elder as Healer with Joan Halifax* (Panacea Productions, 1992)

LAMA TSULTRIM ALLIONE

Books

- *Women of Wisdom* (Routledge & Kegan Paul, 1984; Snow Lion Publications, 2000)
- *Places She Lives* (Penguin, 1999)
- *Feeding Your Demons: Ancient Wisdom for Resolving Inner Conflict* (Little, Brown, 2008)
- *Wisdom Rising: Journey into the Mandala of the Empowered Feminine* (Enliven Books, 2018; also issued as an audiobook by Joan E. Allione, 2018)

Audio

- *Cutting Through Fear* (Sounds True, 2007)
- *Wisdom Rising: Journey into the Mandala of the Empowered Feminine* (Joan E. Allione, 2018)
- *Feeding Your Demons: Ancient Wisdom for Resolving Inner Conflict* (Hachette Audio, 2019)
- *Befriending Your Demons: A Revolutionary Path for Transforming Your Fears and Difficulties into Allies* (Sounds True, 2021)
- *The Empowered Feminine: Meditating with the Dakini Mandala* (Sounds True, 2021)

ANDREW WEIL explored altered states of consciousness in his early publications and later expanded his work to encompass healthy lifestyles and healthcare in general.

Books

- *The Natural Mind: An Investigation of Drugs and the Higher Consciousness* (Houghton Mifflin, 1972; revised edition, 1986)
- *Health and Healing: The Philosophy of Integrative Medicine and Optimum Health* (Houghton Mifflin, 1983; revised edition, 2004)
- *From Chocolate to Morphine: Everything You Need to Know about Mind-altering Drugs* (with Winifred Rosen) (Houghton Mifflin, 1983; revised editions, 1993, 2004)
- *Spontaneous Healing* (Alfred A. Knopf, 1995)
- *Natural Health, Natural Medicine* (Houghton Mifflin, 1995; revised edition, 2004)
- *8 Weeks to Optimum Health: A Proven Program for Taking Full Advantage of Your Body's Natural Healing Power* (Alfred A. Knopf, 1997; revised edition, Ballantine Books, 2007)
- *Eating Well for Optimum Health* (Alfred A. Knopf, 2000)
- *The Healthy Kitchen* (with Rosie Daley) (Alfred A. Knopf, 2002)
- *Healthy Aging* (Alfred A. Knopf, 2005)
- *Why Our Health Matters* (Hudson Street Press, 2009)
- *Spontaneous Happiness* (Little, Brown, 2011)
- *True Food: Seasonal, Sustainable, Simple, Pure* (with Sam Fox and Michael Stebner) (Little, Brown, 2014)
- *Fast Food, Good Food: More Than 150 Quick and Easy Ways to Put Healthy, Delicious Food on the Table* (Little, Brown, 2015)

Audio

- *Mind over Meds: Know When Drugs Are Necessary, When Alternatives Are Better – and When to Let Your Body Heal on Its Own* (Hatchette Audio, 2017)
- *Dr. Andrew Weil's Guide to Optimum Health: A Complete Course on How to Feel Better, Live Longer, and Enhance Your Health - Naturally* (Sounds True, 2015)
- *Taking Care of Yourself: Strategies for Eating Well, Staying Fit, and Living in Balance* (Sounds True, 2015)
- *Meditations for Happiness and Optimum Well Being* (Sounds True, 2014)
- *Eating Well for Optimum Health: The Essential Guide to Food, Diet, and Nutrition* (Random House Audio, 2012)
- *Spontaneous Happiness* (Hatchette Audio, 2011)
- *Breathing: The Master Key to Self Healing* (Sounds True, 2001)

- *Eight Weeks to Optimum Health: A Proven Program for Taking Full Advantage of Your Body's Natural Healing Power* (Random House Audio, 2006)
- *Healthy Aging: A Lifelong Guide to Your Well-Being* (Random House Audio, 2005)

OTHERS

- **Joanna Harcourt-Smith,** *Tripping the Bardo with Timothy Leary: My Psychedelic Love Story* (CreateSpace, 2013)
- **Rosemary Woodruff Leary,** *Psychedelic Refugee: The League for Spiritual Discovery, the 1960s Cultural Revolution, and 23 Years on the Run* (Park Street Press, 2021)
- **Zach Leary,** *And Now the Work Begins: A Manual for Psychedelic Integration Exploring "Set and Setting" in the 21st Century* (Sounds True, 2023)

ACKNOWLEDGMENTS

WE WOULD LIKE TO ACKNOWLEDGE and give thanks to Ram Dass, Timothy Leary, Ralph Metzner, Huston Smith, John Perry Barlow, and Joanna Harcourt-Smith, who have all passed away in the years since the *Dying to Know* film came out. They now know what the Great Mystery of death holds.

Many thanks to Raoul Goff at Mandala Publishing for conceiving of the idea of a Timothy Leary-Ram Dass book, and to all those at Mandala Publishing who contributed to this endeavor. And many thanks to Raghu Markus and Rachael Fisher at the Love Serve Remember Foundation for making it happen.

Deep gratitude to Andrew Ungerleider and the Livingry Foundation for support of the film and this book project.

Many thanks to the angel investors, grants, and in-kind contributions that allowed the film to emerge and evolve organically; and the masterful guidance of Robert Redford, who lent not only his voice narration but more importantly gave very precise notes throughout the editing. Thanks to David Leach, narration writer; the executive producers—Mangusta Productions, Dal LaMagna, Rena Shulsky David & Sami S. David, Sarah Redich Johnson, Celeste Worl & Carla Kleefeld, and Andrew Ungerleider; Michael Donnelly, Ethan Boheme, Dustin Linblad for the mandala imagery, Andreas Reinhart & Mary O'Bierne, David Schlessinger, Threshold Foundation, and David Perez.

And thanks to the organizations, such as Drug Policy Alliance and Multidisciplinary Association of Psychedelic Studies (MAPS), that have been working for decades to bring about a more open acceptance of psychedelic medicines.

Gay Dillingham would personally like to acknowledge the memory of her mother, Ruth Dillingham, who helped every step of the way and passed away on Christmas Eve 2023.

We are especially grateful for those whose shoulders we stand upon, whose heartfelt commitment to freedom and internal growth, and deep reverence for the mystery of life, are helping to awaken humankind and weave the world together.

FOLLOWING PAGE: *Light Work* painting by Autumn Skye.

MANDALA

An Imprint of MandalaEarth
PO Box 3088
San Rafael, CA 94912
www.MandalaEarth.com

Find us on Facebook: www.facebook.com/MandalaEarth

Publisher Raoul Goff
Associate Publisher Phillip Jones
Publishing Director Katie Killebrew
Editorial Assistant Amanda Nelson
VP Creative Director Chrissy Kwasnik
Art Director Ashley Quackenbush
Senior Designer Stephanie Odeh
VP Manufacturing Alix Nicholaeff
Sr Production Manager Joshua Smith
Sr Production Manager, Subsidiary Rights Lina s Palma-Temena

Dying to Know © 2024 Love Serve Remember Foundation & CNS Communications
226 W Ojai Ave Ste. 101 #531, Ojai, CA 93023

Text © 2024 Love Serve Remember Foundation
Images © 2024 Gay Dillingham, Love Serve Remember Foundation, and CNS Communications

To learn more about the film, visit dyingtoknowmovie.com

For more information and teachings, visit RamDass.org
Visit BeHereNowNetwork.com for insightful and entertaining podcasts.
Follow @babaramdass on Instagram, Facebook, TikTok, & X.

ISBN: 979-8-88762-090-9
Manufactured in India by Insight Editions
10 9 8 7 6 5 4 3 2 1

  ROOTS of PEACE   REPLANTED PAPER

Insight Editions, in association with Roots of Peace, will plant two trees for each tree used in the manufacturing of this book. Roots of Peace is an internationally renowned humanitarian organization dedicated to eradicating land mines worldwide and converting war-torn lands into productive farms and wildlife habitats. Roots of Peace will plant two million fruit and nut trees in Afghanistan and provide farmers there with the skills and support necessary for sustainable land use.